My Book

This book belongs to

Name: _____

Copy right © 2019 MATH-KNOTS LLC

All rights reserved, no part of this publication may be reproduced, stored in any system or transmitted in any form, or by any means, electronic, mechanical, photocopying, recording, or otherwise without the written permission of MATH-KNOTS LLC.

Cover Design by :
Gowri Vemuri

First Edition :
April, 2020

Author :
Gowri Vemuri

Editor :
Ritvik Pothapragada

Questions: mathknots.help@gmail.com

NOTE : TJHSST (Thomas Jefferson High School for Science and Technology) or VDOE (Virginia Department of Education) is neither affiliated nor sponsors or endorses this product.

Dedication

This book is dedicated to:

My Mom, who is my best critic, guide and supporter.

To what I am today, and what I am going to become tomorrow,

is all because of your blessings, unconditional affection and support.

This book is dedicated to the

strongest women of my life,

my dearest mom

and

to all those moms in this universe.

G.V.

QUANT - Q

PREFACE

Thomas Jefferson High School for Science and Technology (TJHSST) admission test is based on the below rubric

Test	Math- Quant Q	Reading- Aspire	Science- Aspire
Time	50 minutes	65 minutes	60 minutes
Number of Questions	28	32	40
Measures	• Pattern Recognition • Probability Combinatorics • Out-of-the Box Algebra • Geometry and Optimization	• Key Ideas and Details • Craft and Structure • Integration of Knowledge and Ideas	• Interpretation of Data • Scientific Investigation • Evaluation of Models • Inferences • Experimental Design

    This book (Book 1 Volume 1) helps the students to practice on Pattern recognition, Out of Box algebra and Geometry. Few advanced topics are added as well. Each topic is subdivided into smaller topics with 15 practice questions in each. A total of 1000+ questions to practice for the students.

Book 1 Volume 2 will cover the remaining topics Probability, Combinatorics, Geometry and Optimization.

    Notes on various topics is provided in the beginning of the book and Answer keys in the end.

Visit www.math-knots.com for more practice questions and sample test.

INDEX

Preface	1 - 12
Notes	13 - 32
Formulae	33 - 38
Prime Factors	39 - 41
Numerical expressions	42
Simplify expressions	43
Evaluate expression	44
Exponential expressions	45
Distance between 2 points	46
Midpoint	47 - 50
Equation of a straight line	51
Slope 2 points	52
Slope intercept form	53 - 54
Slope graph	55 - 56
Find the slope	57
Parallel line slope	58
Perpendicular line slope	59
Radicals 1	60 - 62

QUANT - Q

INDEX

Radicals 2	63 - 65
Inequalities	66
One step word problems	67 - 68
Circle area	69 - 70
Volume Sphere	71 - 72
Volume rectangle square prisms	73 - 75
Volume Cone Cylinder	76 - 78
Missing angle 1	79 - 80
Missing angle 2	81 - 82
Reflection	83 - 84
Rotation	85 - 86
Translation	87 - 88
Warm up 1	89 - 94
Practice test 1	95 - 100
Warm up 2	101 - 104
Practice test 2	105 - 110
Warm up 3	111 - 114
Practice test 3	115 - 120

INDEX

Warm up 4	121 - 124
Practice test 4	125 - 130
Warm up 5	131 - 134
Practice test 5	135 - 140
Warm up 6	141 - 144
Practice test 6	145 - 150
Warm up 7	151 - 152
Practice test 7	153 - 158
Answer Keys	159 - 172

NUMBER SYSTEM

Real Numbers:

A number that can be represented on a number line is called a real number.

Rational Numbers (Q):

The numbers can be expressed in the form of $\frac{p}{q}$ (p, q ∈ Z, q ≠ 0) are called Rational numbers.

Irrational Numbers:

The numbers which are not rational numbers are called irrational numbers. i.e., The numbers that cannot be expressed in the form $\frac{p}{q}$ where q is a non zero integer are called irrational numbers.

Example: π

Integers: I or Z = { ……. –3, –2, –1, 0, 1, 2, 3,……}

Whole Numbers: W = {0, 1, 2, 3, 4, 5, 6, …….}

Natural Numbers: N = {1, 2, 3, 4, 5, 6,…….}

Divisibility rules

A number is said to be "divisible" by another if the second number divides evenly into the first. Example, the number 10 is divisible by number 1,2 and 5 evenly into 10.

Divisibility rules #2

1. All even numbers are divisible by 2. Example: Any number ending in 0,2,4,6 or 8.

Divisibility rules #3

1. Add all the digits in the number.

2. If the sum of the digits is divisible by 3, the number is divisible by 3.

3. Example : 13461 : 1 + 3 + 4 + 6 + 1 = 15. 15 is divisible by 3.
   so , 13461 is divisible by 3

Divisibility rules #4

1. Check the last two digits of the given number is divisible by 4 ?

2. If yes, the number is divisible by 4

3. Example : 34336 ends in 36 which is divisible by 4.
   so , 34336 is divisible by 4.

Divisibility rules #5

1. Numbers ending in 5 or 0 are always divisible by 5.

Divisibility rules #6

1. If a number is divisible by 2 and 3, then it is divisible by 6.

Divisibility rules #9
1. Add all the digits in the number.
2. If the sum of the digits is divisible by 9, the number is divisible by 9.
3. Example : 31905 : 3 + 1 + 9 + 0 + 5 = 18. 18 is divisible by 9.
   so , 31905 is divisible by 9.

Divisibility rules #10
1. Any number ending with a digit 0 is divisible by 10.

EXPONENTS PROPERTIES

(1) The square of a real number is always positive.
If $m, n \in Z; a, b \in R \ (a \neq 0)$

(i) $a^{-m} = \dfrac{1}{a^m}$ (ii) $a^m \cdot a^n = a^{m+n}$

(iii) $\dfrac{a^m}{a^n} = a^{m-n}$ (iv) $(a^m)^n = a^{mn}$

(v) $(ab)^m = a^m b^m$ (vi) $\left(\dfrac{a}{b}\right)^m = \dfrac{a^m}{b^m}$ $(b \neq 0)$.

(vii) $\sqrt[n]{a} = a^{1/n}$ (viii) $\sqrt[n]{a^m} = a^{m/n}$

(ix) $\sqrt[n]{\dfrac{a}{b}} = \dfrac{\sqrt[n]{a}}{\sqrt[n]{a}}$ (x) $\sqrt[m]{\sqrt[n]{a}} = a^{\frac{1}{mn}}$

(xi) $a^0 = 1 \ (a \neq 0)$

Example:

Simplify (i) $(27)^{5/3}$.
$(27)^{5/3} = (3^3)^{5/3} = 3^5 = 243.$ $(\because (a^m)^n = a^{mn})$

(ii) $\left(\dfrac{625}{16}\right)^{-5/4} = \left(\dfrac{625}{16}\right)^{-5/4} = \left(\dfrac{16}{625}\right)^{5/4}$ $(\because a^{-m} = \dfrac{1}{a^m})$

$= \left(\dfrac{2^4}{5^4}\right)^{5/4} = \left(\dfrac{2^5}{5^5}\right)$ $\left(\because \left(\dfrac{a}{b}\right)^m = \dfrac{a^m}{b^m}\right)$ $= \left(\dfrac{2}{5}\right)^5$.

InEqualities and Absolute value of a Number:

If x is a real number, then its absolute value or modulus value is denoted by $|x|$ (read as mod x) and defined as follows,

$|x| = x$ when $x > 0$.

$|x| = -x$ when $x < 0$.

$|x| = 0$ when $x = 0$.

For real numbers A and B, an equation as $|A| = B$ when $B = 0$
has 2 solutions $A = B$ or $A = -B$.
If $B < 0$ then $|A| = B$ has no solution.

Set	Notation	Interval Notation
All real numbers between a and b, not including a or b	$\{x|\ a < x < b\}$	(a, b)
All real numbers greater than a, not including a	$\{x|\ x > a\}$	(a, ∞)
All real numbers less than b, not including b	$\{x|\ x < b\}$	$(-\infty, b)$
All real numbers greater than a, including a	$\{x|\ x \geq a\}$	$[a, \infty)$
All real numbers less than b, including b	$\{x|\ x \leq b\}$	$(-\infty, b]$
All real numbers between a and b, including a	$\{x|\ a \leq x < b\}$	$[a, b)$
All real numbers between a and b, including b	$\{x|\ a < x \leq b\}$	$(a, b]$
All real numbers between a and b, including a and b	$\{x|\ a \leq x \leq b\}$	$[a, b]$
All real numbers less than a or greater than b	$\{x|\ x < a$ and $x > b\}$	$(-\infty, a) \cup (b, \infty)$
All real numbers	$\{x|\ x$ is all real numbers$\}$	$(-\infty, \infty)$

Properties of inequalities:

1. Addition property
   If a < b, then a + c < b + c

2. Multiplication property
   If a < b and c > 0, then ac < bc
   If a < b and c < 0, then ac > bc

Example:

The value of $|7| = 7$ ($7 > 0$)

The value of $|-5| = -(-5) = 5$ ($-5 < 0$)

The value of $|x|$ is always positive.

Range of $|x|$ is positive real numbers including zero.

Properties:

(i) If $|x| = a$ then $x = \pm a$.

(ii) If $|x| \leq a$ then $-a \leq x \leq a$.

(iii) If $|x| \geq a$ then $x \leq -a$ or $x \geq a$.

Example 1: If $|x| = 8$, then find the values of x.

Solution: If $|x| = a$; $x = \pm a$
$|x| = 8$, $x = \pm 8$.

Example 2: If $|x| \leq 9$, then find the range of x.

Solution: If $|x| \leq 9$, then $-a \leq x \leq a$
$|x| \leq 9 \Rightarrow -9 \leq x \leq 9$.

Example 3: If $|x| \geq 15$, then find the range of x.

Solution: If $|x| \geq a$, the $x \leq -a$ or $x \geq a$.

$|x| \geq 15 \Rightarrow x \leq -15$ or $x \geq 15$.

Example 4: If $|x+5| = 9$, find the value of x.

Solution: $|x| = a$, then $x = \pm a$

$|x+5| = 9 \Rightarrow x + 5 = \pm 9$.

$x + 5 = 9$ or $x + 5 = -9$

$x = 4$ or $x = -14$.

Example 5: $|3x-7| = 22$, find the value of x.

Solution: $|3x-7| = 22 \Rightarrow 3x - 7 = \pm 22$

$3x - 7 = 22$ or $3x - 7 = -22$

$3x = 29$ or $3x = -22 + 7$

$x = \dfrac{29}{3}$ or $3x = -15 \Rightarrow x = -5$

$x = \dfrac{29}{3}$ or $x = -5$.

Example 6: Solve $|x-5| < 3$.

Solution: $|x| < a \Rightarrow -a < x < a$

$|x-5| < 3 \Rightarrow -3 < x-5 < 3$.

$\Rightarrow -3 + 5 < x < 3 + 5$

$2 < x < 8$.

Example 7: Solve $|3x-10| > 43$.

Solution: $|x| > a \Rightarrow x < -a$ or $x > a$.

$|3x-10| > 43 \Rightarrow 3x - 10 < -43$ or $3x - 10 > 43$.

$3x < -43 + 10$ or $3x > 43 + 10$

$3x < -33$ or $x > \dfrac{53}{3}$.

$x < -11$ or $x > \dfrac{53}{3}$.

Graph of $|x|$:

Since x is any real number, $|x|$ always positive, so graph of $|x|$ belongs to first and second quadrants only.

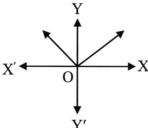

Solving radical equations
An equation containing terms with a variable in the radicand is called a radical equation.

Steps to solve the radical equation :
1. Isolate the radical expression on one side of the equal sign.
2. Move all other terms to other side of the equation.
3. If the radical is a square root , then square both sides of the equation.
   If the radical is a cube root , then rise both sides of the equation to the third power.
   If the radical is a nth root , then rise both sides of the equation to the nth power.
4. If the radical still exists repeat steps 1,2,3. Repeat the process until the radical is eliminated. .
5. Solve the equation.
6. Substitute the solution back for verification.

Solving absolute value equations
The absolute value of x is written as $|x|$. It has the following properties:
If $x \geq 0$, then $|x| = x$.
If $x < 0$, then $|x| = -x$.
For real numbers A and B, an equation of the form $|A| = B$, with $B \geq 0$, will have solutions when $A = B$ or $A = -B$.

If $B < 0$, the equation $|A| = B$ has no solution.
An absolute value equation in the form $|ax + b| = c$ has the following properties:
If $c < 0$, $|ax + b| = c$ has no solution.
If $c = 0$, $|ax + b| = c$ has one solution.
If $c > 0$, $|ax + b| = c$ has two solutions.

1. Isolate the absolute value expression on one side of the equal sign.
2. If $c > 0$, write and solve two equations: *ax+b=c* and *ax+b=−c*.

The Discriminant

The quadratic formula not only gives the solutions to a quadratic equation $ax^2 + bx + c = 0$, but also describes the nature of the solutions. The discriminant, $b^2 - 4ac$ determines whether the solutions are real numbers or complex numbers. Below table describes the properties of the discriminant to the solutions of a quadratic equation.

Value of Discriminant	Results
$b^2 - 4ac = 0$	One rational solution (double solution)
$b^2 - 4ac > 0$, perfect square	Two rational solutions
$b^2 - 4ac > 0$, not a perfect square	Two irrational solutions
$b^2 - 4ac < 0$	Two complex solutions

polynomial equations

A polynomial of degree *n* is an expression of the type

$$a_n x^n + a_{n-1} x^{n-1} + \cdots + a_2 x^2 + a_1 x + a_0$$

where *n* is a positive integer and $a_n, \ldots, a_0$ are real numbers and $a_n \neq 0$.

Setting the polynomial equal to zero gives a **polynomial equation**. The total number of solutions (real and complex) to a polynomial equation is equal to the highest exponent *n*.

Solving Radical Equations:

An equation containing terms with a variable in the radicand is called a **radical equation**.

Given a radical equation, solve it.

1. Isolate the radical expression on one side of the equal sign. Put all remaining terms on the other side.

2. If the radical is a square root, then square both sides of the equation. If It is a cube root, then raise both sides of the equation to the third power. In other words, for an *n* the root radical, raise both sides to the *n*th power. Doing so eliminates the radical symbol.

3. Solve the remaining equation.

4. If a radical term still remains, repeat steps 1–2.

5. Confirm solutions by substituting the min to the original equation.

Set Indicated	Set-Builder Notation	Interval Notation
All real numbers between a and b, but not including a or b	$\{x \mid a < x < b\}$	(a, b)
All real numbers greater than a, but not including a	$\{x \mid x > a\}$	(a, ∞)
All real numbers less than b, but not including b	$\{x \mid x < b\}$	$(-\infty, b)$
All real numbers greater than a, including a	$\{x \mid x \geq a\}$	$[a, \infty)$

Set Indicated	Set-Builder Notation	Interval Notation
All real numbers less than b, including b	$\{x \mid x \leq b\}$	$(-\infty, b]$
All real numbers between a and b, including a	$\{x \mid a \leq x < b\}$	$[a, b)$
All real numbers between a and b, including b	$\{x \mid a < x \leq b\}$	$(a, b]$
All real numbers between a and b, including a and b	$\{x \mid a \leq x \leq b\}$	$[a, b]$
All real numbers less than a or greater than b	$\{x \mid x < a \text{ and } x > b\}$	$(-\infty, a) \cup (b, \infty)$
All real numbers	$\{x \mid x \text{ is all real numbers}\}$	$(-\infty, \infty)$

properties of inequalities

Addition Property   If $a < b$, then $a + c < b + c$.

Multiplication Property   If $a < b$ and $c > 0$, then $ac < bc$.

If $a < b$ and $c < 0$, then $ac > bc$.

These properties also apply to $a \leq b$, $a > b$, and $a \geq b$.

Number series

Sequences of numbers which follow specific patterns are called progression. Depending on the pattern, the progressions are classified as follows.

(i) Arithmetic Progression
(ii) Geometric Progression and
(iii) Harmonic Progression

ARITHMETIC PROGRESSION (A.P.)

Numbers (or terms) are said to be in arithmetic progression when each one, except the first, is obtained by adding a constant to the previous number (or term).

An arithmetic progression can be represented by $a, a + d, a + 2d, …, [a + (n – 1)d]$. Here, d is added to any term to get the next term of the progression. The term a is the first term of the progression, n is the number of terms in the progression and d is the common difference. The nth term is normally represented by T_n and the sum to n terms of an A.P. is denoted by S_n

n^{th} term = $T_n = a + (n – 1)d$

Sum to n terms = $S_n = \left(\dfrac{n}{2}\right)[2a + (n – 1)d]$

The sum to n terms of an A.P. can also be written in a different manner. That is,

sum of n terms = $\left(\dfrac{n}{2}\right)[2a + (n – 1)d] = \left(\dfrac{n}{2}\right)[a + \{a + (n – 1)d\}]$

But, when there are n terms in an A.P., a is the first term and $\{a + (n – 1)d\}$ is the last term. Hence,

$S_n = \left(\dfrac{n}{2}\right)$[first term + last term]

The average of all the terms in an A.P. is called the arithmetic mean (A.M.) of the A.P. Since the average of a certain numbers is equal to the {sum of all the number/number of numbers}.

A.M. of n terms in A.P. = $\frac{S_n}{n} = \frac{1}{n}\left(\frac{n}{2}\right)$

(First Term + Last Term) = $\frac{\text{(First Term + Last Term)}}{2}$

i.e. The A.M. of an A.P. is the average of the first and the last terms of the A.P.

The A.M. of an A.P. can also be obtained by considering any two terms which are EQUIDISTANT from the two ends of the A.P. and taking their average, i.e.

(a) the average of the second term from the beginning and the second term from the end is equal to the A.M. of the A.P.

(b) the average of the third term from the beginning and the third term from the end is also equal to the A.M. of the A.P. and so on.

In general, the average of the kth term from the beginning and the kth term from the end is equal to the A.M. of the A.P.

If the A.M. of an A.P. is known, the sum to n terms of the series (S_n) can be expressed as $S_n = n \,(A.M.)$

In particular, if three numbers are in arithmetic progression, then the middle number is the A.M. i.e. if a, b and c are in A.P., then b is the A.M. of the three terms and $b = \frac{a+c}{2}$.

If a and b are any two numbers, then their A.M. = $\frac{a+b}{2}$.

Note:

(i) If three numbers are in A.P., we can take the three terms to be (a − d), a and (a + d).

(ii) If four numbers are in A.P., we can take the four terms to be (a − 3d), (a − d), (a + d) and (a + 3d). The common difference in this case is 2d and not d.

(iii) If five numbers are in A.P., we can take the five terms to be (a − 2d), (a − d), a, (a + d) and (a + 2d).

Inserting arithmetic mean between two numbers:

When n arithmetic means $a_1, a_2, ..., a_n$ are inserted between a and b, then a, $a_1, a_2, ..., a_n$, b are in A.P.
$t_1 = a$ and $t_{n+2} = b$ of A.P.

The common difference of the A.P. can be obtained as follows:
Given that, n arithmetic means are there between a and b.
$\therefore a = t_1$ and $b = t_{n+2}$
Let d be the common difference.
$b = t_1 + (n + 1)d$
$b = a + (n + 1)d$
$d = \dfrac{(b - a)}{(n + 1)}$

Some important results:

The sum to n terms of the following series are quite useful and, hence, should be remembered by students.

(i) Sum of the first n natural numbers = $\sum_{1}^{n} i = \dfrac{n(n+1)}{2}$

(ii) Sum of squares of the first n natural numbers = $\sum_{1}^{n} i^2 = \dfrac{n(n+1)(2n+1)}{6}$

(iii) Sum of cubes of first n natural numbers

Example 1:

Find the 14th term of an A.P. whose first term is 3 and the common difference is 2.

Solution:

The nth term of an A.P. is given by $t_n = a + (n - 1)d$, where a is the first term and d is the common difference.
$\therefore t_{14} = 3 + (14 - 1)2 = 29$

Example 2:

Find the first term and the common difference of an A.P. if the 3rd term is 6 and the 17th term is 34.

Solution:

If a is the first term and the common difference d, then we have
$a + 2d = 6$ ------- (1)
$a + 16d = 34$ ----- (2)
On subtracting equation (1) from equation (2), we get
$14d = 28 \quad d = 2$
Substituting the value of d in equation (1), we get $a = 2$
$\therefore a = 2$ and $d = 2$

Example 3:

Find the sum of the first 22 terms of an A.P. whose first term is 4 and the common difference is 4/3.

Solution:

Given that, $a = 4$ and $d = \dfrac{4}{3}$.

We have $S_n = \dfrac{n}{2}[2a + (n - 1)d]$

$S_{22} = \left(\dfrac{22}{2}\right)\left[(2)(4) + (22 - 1)\left(\dfrac{4}{3}\right)\right] = (11)(8 + 28) = 396$

Example 4:

Divide 124 into four parts in such a away that they are in A.P. and the product of the first and the 4th part is 128 less than the product of the 2nd and the 3rd parts.

Solution:

Let the four parts be $(a - 3d)$, $(a - d)$, $(a + d)$ and $(a + 3d)$. The sum of these four parts is 124,
i.e. $4a = 124 \quad a = 31$
$(a - 3d)(a + 3d) = (a - d)(a + d) - 128$
$\quad a^2 - 9d^2 = a^2 - d^2 - 128$
$\quad 8d^2 = 128 \quad d = ±4$
As $a = 31$, taking $d = 4$, the four parts are 19, 27, 35 and 43.

Note:

If d is taken as –4, then the same four numbers are obtained, but in decreasing order.

Example 5:

Find the three terms in A.P., whose sum is 36 and product is 960.

Solution:

Let the three terms of an A.P. be $(a - d)$, a and $(a + d)$.
Sum of these terms is $3a$.
$3a = 36 \quad a = 12$
Product of these three terms is
$(a + d) a (a - d) = 960 \quad (12 + d)(12 - d) = 80$
$\quad 144 - d^2 = 80 \quad d = ±8$
Taking $d = 8$, we get the terms as 4, 12 and 20.

Note:

If d is taken as –8, then the same numbers are obtained, but in decreasing order.

Geometric Progression (G.P.):

Numbers are said to be in geometric progression when the ratio of any quantity to the number that follows it is the same. In other words, any term of a G.P. (except the first one) can be obtained by multiplying the previous term by a constant factor.

The constant factor is called the common ratio and is normally represented by r. The first term of a G.P. is generally denoted by a.

A geometric progression can be represented by $a, ar, ar^2, \ldots$ where a is the first term and r is the common ratio of the G.P. n^{th} term of the G.P. is ar^{n-1} i.e. $t_n = ar^{n-1}$

Sum to n terms $= S_n = \dfrac{a(1-r^n)}{1-r} = \dfrac{a(r^n-1)}{r-1} = \dfrac{r(ar^{n-1}) - a}{r-1}$

The sum to n terms of a geometric progression can also be written as

$S_n = \dfrac{r(\text{Last term}) - \text{First term}}{r-1}$

Note:

If n terms $a_1, a_2, a_3, \ldots\ldots a_n$ are in G.P., then the geometric mean (G.M.) of these n terms is given by $= \sqrt[n]{a_1 a_2 a_3 \ldots\ldots a_n}$

If three terms are in geometric progression, then the middle term is the geometric mean of the G.P., i.e. if a, b and c are in G.P., then b is the geometric mean of the three terms.

If there are two terms a and b, their geometric mean is given by G.M. = $\sqrt{ab}$. We see that the 3 terms $a, \sqrt{ab}, b$ are in G.P.

For any two positive numbers a and b, their arithmetic mean is always greater than or equal to their geometric mean, i.e. for any two positive numbers a and b, $\dfrac{a+b}{2} \geq \sqrt{ab}$.

The equality holds if and only if $a = b$.

Infinite geometric progression:

If $-1 < r < 1$ (or $|r| < 1$), then the sum of a geometric progression does not increase infinitely but "converges" to a particular value, no matter how many terms of the G.P. we take. The sum of an infinite geometric progression is represented by S_Π and is given by the formula,

$$S_\Pi = \frac{a}{1-r^2}, \text{ if } |r| < 1.$$

Example 6:

Find the 7th term of the G.P. whose first term is 6 and common ratio is 2/3.

Solution:

Given that, $t_1 = 6$ and $r = \dfrac{2}{3}$

We have $t_n = a \cdot r^{n-1}$

$$t_7 = (6)\left(\frac{2}{3}\right)^6 = \frac{(6)(64)}{729} = \frac{128}{243}$$

Example 7:

Find the common ratio of the G.P. whose first and last terms are 25 and 1/625 respectively and the sum of the G.P. is 19531/625.

Solution:

We know that the sum of a G.P is $\dfrac{\text{first term} - r(\text{last term})}{1-r}$

$$\frac{19531}{625} = \frac{25 - (r/625)}{1-r} \qquad r = 1/5$$

Example 8:

Find three numbers of a G.P. whose sum is 26 and product is 216.

Solution:

Let the three numbers be a/r, a and ar.
Given that,

a/r . a . ar = 216;

$\Rightarrow a^3 = 216; a = 6$
a/r + a + ar = 26
$\Rightarrow 6 + 6r + 6r^2 = 26r$
$\Rightarrow 6r^2 - 20r + 6 = 0$
$\Rightarrow 6r^2 - 18r - 2r + 6 = 0$
$\Rightarrow 6r(r - 3) - 2(r - 3) = 0$
$\Rightarrow r = 1/3$ (or) $r = 3$

Hence the three numbers are 2, 6 and 18 (or) 18, 6 and 2

Example 9:

If $|x| < 1$, then find the sum of the series $2 + 4x + 6x^2 + 8x^3 + \ldots$

Solution:

Let $S = 2 + 4x + 6x^2 + 8x^3 + \ldots$ -------- (1)

$xS = 2x + 4x^2 + 6x^3 + \ldots$ .....(2)

(1) – (2) gives
$S(1 - x) = 2 + 2x + 2x^2 + 2x^3 + \ldots$
$= 2(1 + x + x^2 + \ldots)$

$1 + x + x^2 + \ldots$ is an infinite G.P with a = 1, r = x and $|r| = |x| < 1$

∴ Sum of the series = $1/(1 - x)$

∴ $S(1 - x) = 2/(1 - x)$

∴ $S = 2/(1 - x)^2$

Example 10:

Find the sum of the series $1, 2/5, 4/25, 8/125, \ldots \infty$.

Solution:

Given that, $a = 1$, $r = \dfrac{2}{5}$ and $|r| = \left|\dfrac{2}{5}\right| < 1$

$\therefore S_\infty = \dfrac{a}{1-r} = \dfrac{1}{1-\dfrac{2}{5}} = 5/3$

Note:

When n geometric means are there between a and b, the common ratio of the G.P. can be derived as follows.

Given that, n geometric means are there between a and b.
$\therefore a = t_1$ and $b = t_{n+2}$
Let 'r' be the common ratio
$\quad b = (t_1)(r^{n+1}) \quad b = a\, r^{n+1}$
$\quad r^{n+1} = \dfrac{b}{a}$

$\quad r = \sqrt[(n+1)]{\dfrac{b}{a}}$

Harmonic Progression (H.P.):

A progression is said to be a harmonic progression if the reciprocal of the terms in the progression form an arithmetic progression.
For example, consider the series

$\dfrac{1}{2}, \dfrac{1}{5}, \dfrac{1}{8}, \dfrac{1}{11}, \ldots$

The progression formed by taking reciprocals of terms of the above series is 2, 5, 8, 11,.... Clearly, these terms form an A.P. whose common difference is 3.

n^{th} term of an H.P:

We know that if a, a + d, a + 2d,….are in A.P., then the nth term of this A.P. is a + (n – 1) d. Its reciprocal is

$$\frac{1}{a+(n-1)d}$$

So, n^{th} term of an H.P. whose first two terms are $\frac{1}{a}$ and $\frac{1}{a+d}$ is $\frac{1}{a+(n-1)d}$

Note:

There is no concise general formula for the sum to n terms of an H.P.

Example 11:

Find the 10th term of the H.P. $\frac{3}{2}, 1, \frac{3}{4}, \frac{3}{5}, \ldots\ldots$

Solution:

The given H.P. is $\frac{3}{2}, 1, \frac{3}{4}, \frac{3}{5}, \ldots$

The corresponding A.P. is $\frac{2}{3}, 1, \frac{4}{3}, \frac{5}{3}, \ldots$

Here a = $\frac{2}{3}$; d = $1 - \frac{2}{3} = \frac{1}{3}$

∴ T_{10} of the corresponding A.P. is a + (10 – 1)d = $\frac{2}{3} + (9)\frac{1}{3} = \frac{11}{3}$

Hence required term in H.P. is $\frac{3}{11}$

Harmonic Mean (H.M.):

If three terms are in H.P., then the middle term is the H.M. of other two terms.

The harmonic mean of two terms a and b is given by

$$H.M. = \frac{2ab}{a+b}$$

Relation between A.M., H.M. and G.M. of two numbers

Let x and y be two numbers

$\therefore$ A.M. $= \dfrac{x+y}{2}$, G.M. $= \sqrt{xy}$ and H.M. $= \dfrac{2xy}{x+y}$

(A.M.) (H.M.) = (G.M)^2

Inserting n harmonic means between two numbers:

To insert n H.M.'s between two numbers, we first take the corresponding arithmetic series and insert n arithmetic means, and next, we find the corresponding harmonic series.

This is illustrated by the example below:

Example 12:

Insert three harmonic means between $\dfrac{1}{12}$ and $\dfrac{1}{20}$

Solution:

After inserting the harmonic means let the harmonic progression be

$\dfrac{1}{a}, \dfrac{1}{a+d}, \dfrac{1}{a+2d}, \dfrac{1}{a+3d}, \dfrac{1}{a+4d}$

As $\dfrac{1}{a} = \dfrac{1}{12}$ and $\dfrac{1}{a+4d} = \dfrac{1}{20}$ a = 12 and d = 2

$\therefore$ The required harmonic means are $\dfrac{1}{14}, \dfrac{1}{16}$ and $\dfrac{1}{18}$

FORMULA SHEET

1. Area of a triangle

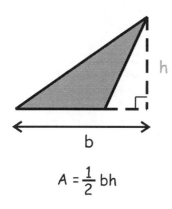

$A = \frac{1}{2} bh$

2. Area of a parellelogram

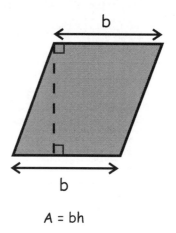

$A = bh$

3. Volume and Surface area of a Cuboid

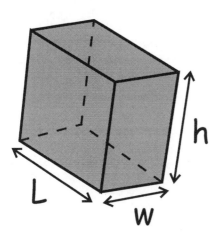

$V = lwh$
$S.A = 2(lw + lh + wh)$

4. volume and Surface area of a Cone

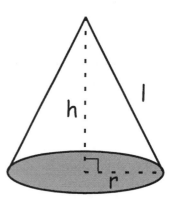

$V = \frac{1}{3} \Pi r^2$
$S.A = \Pi r(l + h)$

QUANT - Q

FORMULAE

5. Perimeter and Area of a Square

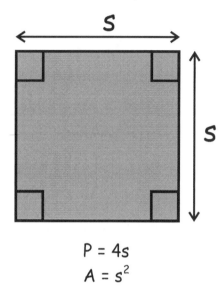

$P = 4s$
$A = s^2$

6. Area of a Trapezium

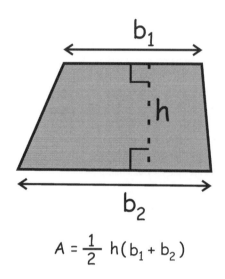

$A = \frac{1}{2} h(b_1 + b_2)$

7. Volume and Surface area of a Cylinder

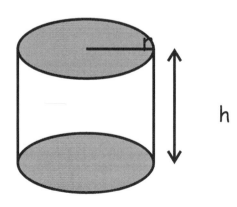

$V = \Pi r^2 h$
$S.A = 2\Pi r(h+r)$

8. Volume and Surface area of a Pyramid

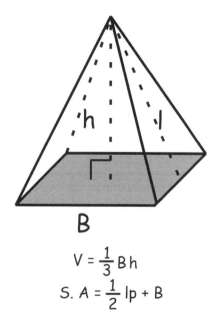

$V = \frac{1}{3} Bh$
$S.A = \frac{1}{2} lp + B$

QUANT - Q

FORMULAE

9. Circumference and Area of a Circle

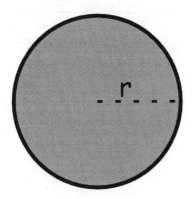

$c = \pi r$
$A = \pi r^2$

pi
$\pi = 3.14$
$\pi = \dfrac{22}{7}$

10. Right angled Triangle (Pythagoran)

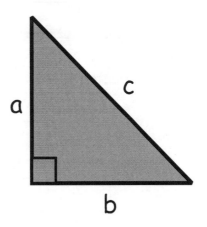

$c^2 = a^2 + b^2$

Pythagorean triplets
Examples : (3 , 4 , 5)
(5 , 12 , 13)
(7 , 24 , 25)
(15 , 20 , 25)
(6 , 8 , 10)
(9 , 12 , 15)
(6 , 8 , 10)
(12 , 16 , 20)
(10 , 24 , 26)

11. Perimeter and Area of a Rectangle

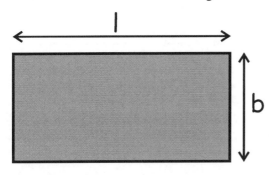

Area = l b x
Perimeter = 2(l + b)

©All rights reserved-Math-Knots LLC., VA-USA   www.math-knots.com

QUANT - Q

12. Quadratic formula

$$x = \frac{-b \pm \sqrt{b^2 - 4ac}}{2a}$$

13. Algebraic Identities

$$(a + b)^2 = a^2 + 2ab + b^2$$

$$(a - b)^2 = a^2 - 2ab + b^2$$

$$a^2 - b^2 = (a + b)(a - b)$$

$$a^2 + b^2 = (a + b)^2 - 2ab$$

$$a^2 + b^2 = (a - b)^2 + 2ab$$

14. Equation of a Straight line

Slope intercept form
$y = mx + c$
Where m = slope
c = y - intercept

Point slope form
$y - y_1 = m(x - x_1)$
Where m = slope
Straight line passes through the point (x_1, y_1)

15. Distance between 2 points

$P(x_1, y_1) \quad Q(x_2, y_2)$

$$PQ = \sqrt{(x_2 - x_1)^2 + (y_2 - y_1)^2}$$

16. Slope between 2 points (st line)

$P(x_1, y_1) \quad Q(x_2, y_2)$

$$\text{Slope} = \frac{y_2 - y_1}{x_2 - x_1}$$

QUANT - Q

FORMULAE

Abbreviations

milligram	mg
gram	g
kilogram	kg
milliliter	mL
liter	L
kiloliter	kL
millimeter	mm
centimeter	cm
meter	m
kilometer	km
square centimeter	cm^2
cubic centimeter	cm^3

volume	V
total Square Area	S.A
area of base	B
ounce	oz
pound	lb
quart	qt
gallon	gal.
inches	in.
foot	ft
yard	yd
mile	mi.
square inch	sq in.
square foot	sq ft
cubic inch	cu in.
cubic foot	cu ft

year	yr
month	mon
hour	hr
minute	min
second	sec

QUANT Q PATTERN RECOGNITION Vol 1

Prime Factors #1

Write the prime factorization of each number given below.

1. 36

    (A) 5 · 7   (B) 2 · 2   (C) 2 · 2 · 3 · 3   (D) 3 · 7

2. 20

    (A) 2 · 2 · 2 · 2   (B) 2 · 7   (C) 2 · 2 · 5   (D) 3 · 7

3. -37

    (A) -37   (B) -2 · 2 · 2 · 3 · 37   (C) -2 · 2 · 37   (D) -2 · 2 · 2 · 3 · 3 · 37

4. -71

    (A) -71   (B) -2 · 2 · 2 · 3 · 3 · 71   (C) -2 · 2 · 2 · 3 · 71   (D) -2 · 2 · 2 · 71

5. -35

    (A) -5 · 7   (B) -2 · 5 · 5 · 7   (C) -2 · 2 · 2 · 3 · 5 · 5 · 7   (D) -2 · 2 · 5 · 5 · 7

6. 38

    (A) 2 · 3 · 3   (B) 2 · 3   (C) 2 · 5   (D) 2 · 19

7. -66

    (A) -2 · 3 · 11   (B) -2 · 3 · 3 · 5 · 11   (C) -2 · 2 · 3 · 3 · 3 · 5 · 11   (D) -2 · 3 · 3 · 11

8. 80

    (A) 2 · 3 · 3 · 5   (B) 3 · 3 · 3 · 3   (C) 2 · 3 · 23   (D) 2 · 2 · 2 · 2 · 5

Numerical Expressions #2

Evaluate the below numerical expressions.

1) $((41)(5) - (-19)) \div 14$
   A) 35   B) -16
   C) 16   D) 23

2) $11 - (9)(4^2)$
   A) −133   B) −150
   C) −153   D) −134

3) $((24 - 7) \div (-17))(-20)$
   A) 5   B) 0
   C) 31   D) 20

4) $((-6) + 1 - 15)(10)$
   A) −204   B) 200
   C) −200   D) −193

5) $(-11) \div (3 - 14) - 17$
   A) −16   B) 2
   C) −35   D) 16

6) $(-9) - 10 + 8 - 4$
   A) −15   B) −10
   C) −17   D) 16

7) $3 + (-20) + 3^2$
   A) −8   B) −26
   C) −24   D) 28

8) $(((-56) \div (-8)) - (-16))(-2)$
   A) −46   B) −55
   C) −66   D) 46

Simplify the below expressions.

1. $-3(1+3b) - 6(b-5)$

   (A) 27 - 15b (B) 27 - 2b (C) -9 + 35b (D) -150b + 6

2. $-13(-5-5n) - 5(6n-4)$

   (A) -33 - 99n (B) -11n - 58 (C) 85 + 44n (D) 85 + 35n

3. $-4(2+5x) - 6(x-2)$

   (A) 4 - 26x (B) 4 - 37x (C) 22 - 107x (D) 38x + 115

4. $-11(x+12) - 13(2x-4)$

   (A) -37x - 80 (B) -6x + 52 (C) -16x + 52 (D) 7 - 70x

5. $-5(r+9) - 12(-4-11r)$

   (A) 106r + 3 (B) 103r + 3 (C) 127r + 3 (D) 114r + 3

6. $-3(1-6p) - 6(12-10p)$

   (A) -86p - 99 (B) -75 + 80p (C) -75 + 78p (D) -78 + 24p

7. $-11(1+7v) - 4(1-14v)$

   (A) -15 - 21v (B) -31v + 124 (C) -18v - 6 (D) -12v - 6

8. $-9(b-11) - (13b+14)$

   (A) -22b + 85 (B) -132b - 139 (C) -123b - 139 (D) -111b - 139

Evaluate Expressions #4

Evaluate the below expressions.

1. $7 + p - m$; where $m = -8$, $p = 7$

   (A) 25   (B) 26   (C) 22   (D) 20

2. $c + a - c$; where $a = -4$, and $c = -10$

   (A) -4 (B) -2 (C) -13 (D) 4

3. $|n| + m$; where $m = 9$, and $n = -1$

   (A) 8   (B) 16   (C) 10   (D) 17

4. $\dfrac{z}{4} + x$; where $x = -8$, and $z = -8$

   (A) -10 (B) 0   (C) -6 (D) -2

5. $y(z + y)$; where $y = 2$, and $z = 6$

   (A) 24   (B) 16   (C) 12   (D) 15

6. xy^3; where $x = -1$, and $y = 4$

   (A) -64 (B) -70 (C) -66 (D) -72

7. $(x + y)^2$; where $x = 7$, and $y = -3$

   (A) 26   (B) 22   (C) 6   (D) 16

8. $-3m + n$; where $m = -3$, and $n = 10$

   (A) 19   (B) 24   (C) 26   (D) 14

QUANT Q PATTERN RECOGNITION Vol 1

Exponential Expressions #5

Simplify the below with positive exponents.

1) $\dfrac{2x^5 y^3}{(x^2)^0}$

  A) $\dfrac{2}{x^{25} y^{16}}$ B) $16x^{19} y^{16}$
  C) $2x^5 y^3$ D) $\dfrac{8}{y^6}$

2) $\dfrac{(2xy)^2}{2y^4}$

  A) $\dfrac{1}{4x^2 y}$ B) $\dfrac{1}{32x^3 y^{18}}$
  C) $\dfrac{y}{4x}$ D) $\dfrac{2x^2}{y^2}$

3) $\dfrac{(2m^5)^5}{m^4}$

  A) $\dfrac{1}{4m^{10} n^4}$ B) $32m^{21}$
  C) $\dfrac{n^{20}}{m^{12}}$ D) $\dfrac{m^{16}}{2}$

4) $\dfrac{y^4}{(2x^2 y^3)^5}$

  A) $\dfrac{x^{11} y^8}{2}$ B) $\dfrac{1}{4x^7 y^4}$
  C) $\dfrac{1}{2x^2 y^5}$ D) $\dfrac{1}{32x^{10} y^{11}}$

5) $\dfrac{(2x^4 y^3)^4}{x^3 y^3}$

  A) $\dfrac{1}{yx^5}$ B) $16x^{13} y^9$
  C) $\dfrac{1}{x^4 y^4}$ D) $\dfrac{4y^{12}}{x^3}$

6) $\dfrac{x^3}{(x^4 y^5)^4}$

  A) $x^{20} y^9$ B) $\dfrac{x}{y^7}$
  C) $\dfrac{1}{x^{13} y^{20}}$ D) $16y^2 x^7$

7) $\dfrac{(2vu^4)^2}{u}$

  A) $16v^4 u^6$ B) $\dfrac{1}{32u^{19}}$
  C) $4v^2 u^7$ D) $\dfrac{8}{u^3}$

8) $\dfrac{x^3 y^4}{(2x^3 y^2)^2}$

  A) $\dfrac{1}{4x^8 y^3}$ B) $16x^{24} y^{16}$
  C) $\dfrac{1}{2x^2 y^4}$ D) $\dfrac{1}{4x^3}$

Find the distance between the below points.

1. A(4, 6), B(−4, −8)

   (A) $2\sqrt{65}$ (B) $\sqrt{6}$ (C) $\sqrt{22}$ (D) 2

2. C(−2, 5), D(−4, −2)

   (A) $3\sqrt{5}$ (B) $\sqrt{53}$ (C) $3\sqrt{3}$ (D) 3

3. E(4, 5), F(8, 3)

   (A) $2\sqrt{5}$ (B) $4\sqrt{5}$ (C) $4\sqrt{13}$ (D) $\sqrt{6}$

4. G(−7, 1), H(−6, −1)

   (A) 13   (B) $\sqrt{5}$ (C) $\sqrt{13}$ (D) $\sqrt{3}$

5. I(−7, −7), J(1, −1)

   (A) $\sqrt{22}$ (B) 10   (C) $\sqrt{10}$ (D) 5

6. K(−8, −7), L(−7, −1)

   (A) 17   (B) $\sqrt{7}$ (C) $2\sqrt{2}$ (D) $\sqrt{37}$

7. M(4, 4), N(6, −6)

   (A) $2\sqrt{22}$ (B) $4\sqrt{6}$ (C) $2\sqrt{26}$ (D) $\sqrt{51}$

Find the midpoint of each line segment given in below graphs.

1.

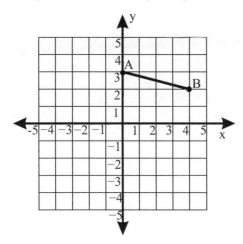

(A) (1.5, 3)   (B) (−2, 0.5)   (C) (8, 1)   (D) (2, 1.5)

2.

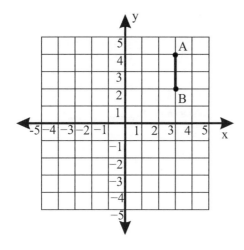

(A) (3.5, 2.5)   (B) (0, 1)   (C) (3, 0)   (D) (3, 3)

Find the midpoint of each line segment given in below graphs.

3.

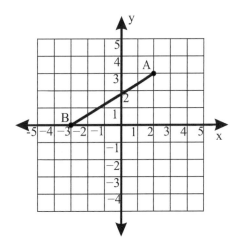

(A) (−2.5, −1.5)   (B) (−0.5, 1.5)   (C) (−1.5, 2.5)   (D) (7, 6)

4.

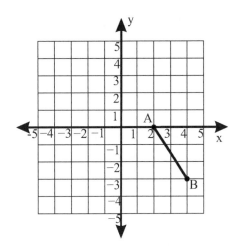

(A) (3, −1.5)   (B) (1, 0.5)   (C) (6, −6)   (D) (−1, 1.5)

Find the midpoint of each line segment given in below graphs.

5.

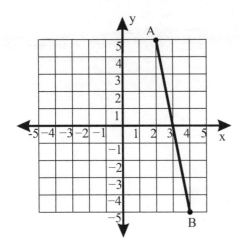

(A) (3, 0)   (B) (−0.5, 3.5)   (C) (0, 15)   (D) (1, −5)

6.

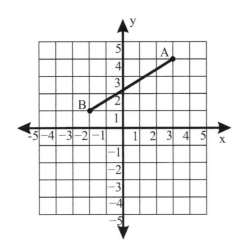

(A) (−2.5, −1.5)   (B) (−0.5, 3.5)   (C) (8, 7)   (D) (0.5, 2.5)

Find the midpoint of each line segment given in below graphs.

7.

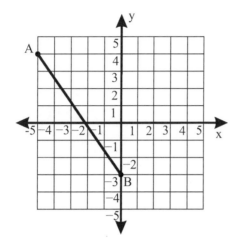

(A) (−1.5, −0.5) (B) (−10, 11) (C) (−2.5, 0.5) (D) (2.5, −3.5)

8.

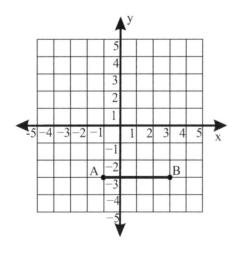

(A) (7, −3) (B) (0, 1) (C) (−2, 0) (D) (1, −3)

Equation of a straight line #8

Write the standard form of the straight line passing through the given points below.

1. A(2, 4) and B(0, −3)

    (A) 2x + 5y = 7   (B) 10x + 2y = −7   (C) 7x − 2y = 6   (D) 2x + 7y = 10

2. C(0, 2) and D(1, 4)

    (A) 2x + 2y = −1   (B) 2x − y = −2   (C) 4x + y = −1   (D) 5x − y = −1

3. E(2, −5) and F(0, −5)

    (A) 5x = 1   (B) x + 2y = 0   (C) y = −5   (D) 2x = 1

4. G(3, −1) and H(−2, 0)

    (A) x − 5y = −2   (B) 5x − y = 2   (C) x + y = 3   (D) x + 5y = −2

5. I(3, −4) and J(0, −1)

    (A) 4x + 3y = −1   (B) x + y = −1   (C) 3x + 3y = 1   (D) 3x − y = 4

6. K(0, 2) and L(5, −2)

    (A) 4x − 5y = −4   (B) 5x − 4y = 10   (C) 4x + 5y = −4   (D) 4x + 5y = 10

7. M(0, 4) and N(2, −2)

    (A) 3x + y = 4   (B) x − y = −5   (C) x − y = 2   (D) x + y = 2

Find the slope of the straight line passing through the points given below.

1. A(18, −15), B(18, −17)

   (A) Undefined (B) −1
   (C) 1 (D) 0

2. M(−9, −14), N(−9, 7)

   (A) $-\dfrac{5}{2}$ (B) Undefined
   (C) 0 (D) $\dfrac{5}{2}$

3. O(−1, 1), P(−15, −1)

   (A) $-\dfrac{1}{7}$ (B) $\dfrac{1}{7}$
   (C) −7 (D) 7

4. Q(−1, 9), R(9, −6)

   (A) $\dfrac{2}{3}$ (B) $-\dfrac{2}{3}$
   (C) $-\dfrac{3}{2}$ (D) $\dfrac{3}{2}$

5. S(−17, 20), T(−16, −17)

   (A) −37 (B) $-\dfrac{1}{37}$
   (C) $\dfrac{1}{37}$ (D) 37

6. U(−6, 12), V(−6, 8)

   (A) −1 (B) 1
   (C) Undefined (D) 0

QUANT Q OUT OF BOX ALGEBRA Vol 1

Slope intercept form #10

Find the slope-intercept form of the straight line with the given slope and y-intercept for all the problems given below.

1. Slope = $-\frac{2}{5}$, y-intercept = 5

   (A) $y = -5x - \frac{2}{5}$
   (B) $y = x + 5 - \frac{2}{5}$
   (C) $y = 5x - \frac{2}{5}$
   (D) $y = -\frac{2}{5}x - 5$

2. Slope = $\frac{7}{4}$, y-intercept = 5

   (A) $y = x + 5$
   (B) $y = 5x + 1$
   (C) $y = \frac{7}{4}x + 5$
   (D) $y = -x + 1$

3. Slope = $-\frac{9}{4}$, y-intercept = -4

   (A) $y = -4x + \frac{1}{2}$
   (B) $y = -\frac{9}{4}x - 4$
   (C) $y = -\frac{1}{2}x - 4$
   (D) $y = \frac{1}{2}x - 4$

4. Slope = -3, y-intercept = 5

   (A) $y = -3x + 5$
   (B) $y = 5x - 3$
   (C) $y = -5x - 3$
   (D) $y = -3x - 5$

Find the slope-intercept form of the straight line with the given slope and y-intercept for all the problems given below.

5. | Slope = 6, y-intercept = 3 |

   (A) $y = -5x - 6$ (B) $y = 3x - 6$

   (C) $y = -6x + 3$ (D) $y = 6x + 3$

6. | Slope = $\dfrac{3}{5}$, y-intercept = -4 |

   (A) $y = \dfrac{3}{5}x + 4$ (B) $y = 4x + \dfrac{3}{5}$

   (C) $y = \dfrac{3}{5}x - 4$ (D) $y = -4x + \dfrac{3}{5}$

7. | Slope = $\dfrac{1}{2}$, y-intercept = -3 |

   (A) $y = -3x - \dfrac{1}{2}$ (B) $y = -2x - 3$

   (C) $y = x - 3 - \dfrac{1}{2}$ (D) $y = \dfrac{1}{2}x - 3$

Find the slope of the straight line for each of the questions below.

1)

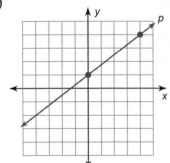

A) $\dfrac{4}{3}$ B) $\dfrac{3}{4}$

C) $-\dfrac{4}{3}$ D) $-\dfrac{3}{4}$

2)

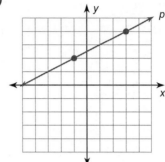

A) 2   B) $\dfrac{1}{2}$

C) −2   D) $-\dfrac{1}{2}$

3)

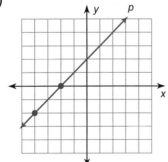

A) $-\dfrac{4}{5}$ B) 1

C) −1   D) $\dfrac{4}{5}$

4)

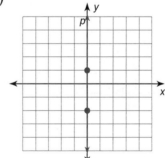

A) $\dfrac{3}{4}$ B) $-\dfrac{3}{4}$

C) 0   D) Undefined

Find the slope of the straight line for each of the questions below.

5)

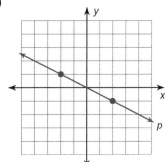

A) $\dfrac{1}{2}$ B) $-\dfrac{1}{2}$
C) -2 D) 2

6)

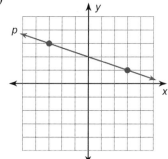

A) 3 B) $\dfrac{1}{3}$
C) -3 D) $-\dfrac{1}{3}$

7)

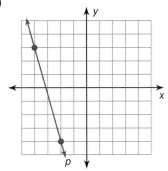

A) $\dfrac{7}{2}$ B) $-\dfrac{7}{2}$
C) $-\dfrac{2}{7}$ D) $\dfrac{2}{7}$

8)

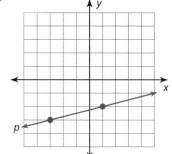

A) $\dfrac{1}{4}$ B) -4
C) 4 D) $-\dfrac{1}{4}$

Find the slope #12

Find the slope of the straight line for each of the questions below.

1) $x + y = -3$
   A) -1 B) 1
   C) $\dfrac{3}{2}$ D) $-\dfrac{3}{2}$

2) $4x + 3y = 3$
   A) $-\dfrac{4}{3}$ B) $-\dfrac{3}{4}$
   C) $\dfrac{3}{4}$ D) $\dfrac{4}{3}$

3) $2x - 3y = 6$
   A) $\dfrac{2}{3}$ B) $-\dfrac{2}{3}$
   C) $\dfrac{3}{2}$ D) $-\dfrac{3}{2}$

4) $3x - 5y = -10$
   A) $\dfrac{5}{3}$ B) $-\dfrac{5}{3}$
   C) $-\dfrac{3}{5}$ D) $\dfrac{3}{5}$

5) $5x + 2y = 0$
   A) $-\dfrac{5}{2}$ B) $-\dfrac{2}{5}$
   C) $\dfrac{5}{2}$ D) $\dfrac{2}{5}$

6) $4x + y = 1$
   A) 4 B) $\dfrac{1}{4}$
   C) $-\dfrac{1}{4}$ D) -4

7) $x + 2y = 6$
   A) 2 B) $\dfrac{1}{2}$
   C) $-\dfrac{1}{2}$ D) -2

8) $5x - 3y = -12$
   A) $-\dfrac{5}{3}$ B) $\dfrac{3}{5}$
   C) $\dfrac{5}{3}$ D) $-\dfrac{3}{5}$

Parallel line slope #13

Find the slope of a line parallel to each given line.

1) $y = -5$
   A) -2 B) Undefined
   C) 0 D) 2

2) $5x - 4y = 0$
   A) $\dfrac{5}{4}$ B) $\dfrac{4}{5}$
   C) $-\dfrac{5}{4}$ D) $-\dfrac{4}{5}$

3) $x = 1$
   A) Undefined B) $-\dfrac{1}{2}$
   C) 0 D) $\dfrac{1}{2}$

4) $x + 5y = 0$
   A) $\dfrac{1}{5}$ B) 5
   C) $-\dfrac{1}{5}$ D) -5

5) $x - 4y = -20$
   A) -4 B) 4
   C) $\dfrac{1}{4}$ D) $-\dfrac{1}{4}$

6) $x + 4y = -16$
   A) 4 B) $-\dfrac{1}{4}$
   C) $\dfrac{1}{4}$ D) -4

7) $5x - 3y = -9$
   A) $-\dfrac{3}{5}$ B) $-\dfrac{5}{3}$
   C) $\dfrac{5}{3}$ D) $\dfrac{3}{5}$

8) $3x + 2y = 4$
   A) $-\dfrac{3}{2}$ B) $-\dfrac{2}{3}$
   C) $\dfrac{3}{2}$ D) $\dfrac{2}{3}$

Find the slope of a line perpendicular to each given line.

1) $y = -3x + 2$

   A) $\dfrac{1}{3}$ B) 3

   C) -3 D) $-\dfrac{1}{3}$

2) $y = -\dfrac{4}{5}x - 3$

   A) $\dfrac{4}{5}$ B) $\dfrac{5}{4}$

   C) $-\dfrac{5}{4}$ D) $-\dfrac{4}{5}$

3) $y = -4x + 4$

   A) -4 B) $\dfrac{1}{4}$

   C) $-\dfrac{1}{4}$ D) 4

4) $y = -\dfrac{3}{2}x - 4$

   A) $\dfrac{3}{2}$ B) $-\dfrac{2}{3}$

   C) $-\dfrac{3}{2}$ D) $\dfrac{2}{3}$

5) $y = -\dfrac{5}{2}x + 2$

   A) $\dfrac{5}{2}$ B) $\dfrac{2}{5}$

   C) $-\dfrac{5}{2}$ D) $-\dfrac{2}{5}$

6) $y = x - 1$

   A) -1 B) 1

   C) $-\dfrac{2}{3}$ D) $\dfrac{2}{3}$

7) $y = \dfrac{6}{5}x + 1$

   A) $-\dfrac{5}{6}$ B) $-\dfrac{6}{5}$

   C) $\dfrac{6}{5}$ D) $\dfrac{5}{6}$

8) $y = 3x + 4$

   A) $-\dfrac{1}{3}$ B) $\dfrac{1}{3}$

   C) 3 D) -3

Simplify the below radicals.

1. $\dfrac{-7-\sqrt{2}}{7+\sqrt{6}}$

   (A) $\dfrac{-35+7\sqrt{6}-5\sqrt{2}+2\sqrt{3}}{19}$ (B) $\dfrac{-49+7\sqrt{6}+14\sqrt{2}-4\sqrt{3}}{43}$

   (C) $\dfrac{-49+7\sqrt{6}-7\sqrt{2}+2\sqrt{3}}{43}$ (D) $\dfrac{-63+7\sqrt{6}-9\sqrt{2}-2\sqrt{3}}{75}$

2. $\dfrac{5-\sqrt{5}}{3-6\sqrt{2}}$

   (A) $\dfrac{-5-10\sqrt{2}+\sqrt{5}+2\sqrt{10}}{21}$ (B) $\dfrac{-5-120\sqrt{2}+2\sqrt{5}+48\sqrt{10}}{1151}$

   (C) $\dfrac{-5+10\sqrt{2}-\sqrt{5}+2\sqrt{10}}{21}$ (D) $\dfrac{-2+10\sqrt{2}+\sqrt{5}+2\sqrt{10}}{27}$

3. $\dfrac{-10-\sqrt{10}}{10+\sqrt{6}}$

   (A) $\dfrac{-60+5\sqrt{6}-6\sqrt{10}+\sqrt{15}}{69}$ (B) $\dfrac{-100+10\sqrt{6}-10\sqrt{13}+\sqrt{78}}{94}$

   (C) $\dfrac{-50+5\sqrt{6}-10\sqrt{3}+3\sqrt{2}}{47}$ (D) $\dfrac{-50+5\sqrt{6}-5\sqrt{10}+\sqrt{15}}{47}$

Simplify the below radicals.

4. $$\dfrac{10\sqrt{5} - 2\sqrt{7}}{2 - 2\sqrt{3}}$$

   (A) $\dfrac{-12\sqrt{5} + 8\sqrt{7}}{5}$ (B) $\dfrac{-5\sqrt{5} - 5\sqrt{15} + \sqrt{7} + \sqrt{21}}{2}$

   (C) $\dfrac{-5\sqrt{5} - 5\sqrt{15}}{2}$ (D) $\dfrac{-6\sqrt{5} + 6\sqrt{15} - \sqrt{7} - \sqrt{21}}{75}$

5. $$\dfrac{-4 + \sqrt{7}}{4\sqrt{5} - \sqrt{6}}$$

   (A) $\dfrac{-28\sqrt{5} - 4\sqrt{6} + 7\sqrt{35} + \sqrt{42}}{47}$ (B) $\dfrac{-16\sqrt{5} - 4\sqrt{6} + 4\sqrt{35} + \sqrt{42}}{74}$

   (C) $\dfrac{-8\sqrt{5} - 2\sqrt{6} + 10\sqrt{2} + \sqrt{15}}{37}$ (D) $\dfrac{-11\sqrt{5} - 4\sqrt{6} + 13\sqrt{33} + \sqrt{43}}{74}$

6. $$\dfrac{8}{9\sqrt{3} - 5\sqrt{5}}$$

   (A) $\sqrt{5}$ (B) $\dfrac{36\sqrt{3} + 20\sqrt{5}}{59}$

   (C) $\dfrac{-48\sqrt{3} - 40\sqrt{5}}{17}$ (D) $\dfrac{36\sqrt{13} + 20\sqrt{5}}{59}$

Simplify the below radicals.

7. $\dfrac{7 + 6\sqrt{10}}{\sqrt{3} + 4}$

(A) $\dfrac{-7\sqrt{3} + 28 - 6\sqrt{30} + 24\sqrt{10}}{13}$

(B) $\dfrac{-7\sqrt{3} + 28 - 5\sqrt{30} + 20\sqrt{10}}{13}$

(C) $\dfrac{-7\sqrt{3} + 42 - 6\sqrt{30} + 36\sqrt{10}}{33}$

(D) $\dfrac{-7\sqrt{3} + 28 - 8\sqrt{2} + 18\sqrt{10}}{13}$

Simplify the below to the lowest positive terms.

1. $$\frac{\sqrt{40x^2y^2}}{9\sqrt{35x^4y^4}}$$

   (A) $\dfrac{2\sqrt{14}}{77xy}$ (B) $\dfrac{2\sqrt{14}}{63xy}$

   (C) $\dfrac{2\sqrt{95}}{171xy}$ (D) $\dfrac{\sqrt{14}}{28xy}$

2. $$\frac{9\sqrt{3x^3y^2}}{9\sqrt{6x^2y^4}}$$

   (A) $\dfrac{\sqrt{30x}}{6y}$ (B) $\dfrac{7\sqrt{2x}}{18y}$

   (C) $\dfrac{\sqrt{2x}}{2y}$ (D) $\dfrac{\sqrt{2x}}{3y}$

3. $$\frac{5\sqrt{5p^3}}{\sqrt{7p^3}}$$

   (A) $\dfrac{5\sqrt{35}}{7}$ (B) $\dfrac{5\sqrt{10}}{4}$

   (C) $\dfrac{5\sqrt{2}}{2}$ (D) $\dfrac{5\sqrt{2}}{3}$

Simplify the below to the lowest positive terms.

4. $$\frac{\sqrt{10x^2}}{\sqrt{7x^3}}$$

    (A) $\dfrac{\sqrt{5x}}{2x}$
    (B) $\dfrac{\sqrt{10x}}{3x}$

    (C) $\dfrac{\sqrt{70x}}{7x}$
    (D) $\dfrac{\sqrt{10x}}{2x}$

5. $$\frac{8\sqrt{9n}}{\sqrt{2n^2}}$$

    (A) $\dfrac{15\sqrt{2n}}{n}$
    (B) $\dfrac{12\sqrt{2n}}{n}$

    (C) $\dfrac{24\sqrt{n}}{n}$
    (D) $\dfrac{27\sqrt{2n}}{2n}$

6. $$\frac{\sqrt{8p}}{7\sqrt{7p^2}}$$

    (A) $\dfrac{\sqrt{14p}}{28p}$
    (B) $\dfrac{2\sqrt{14p}}{49p}$

    (C) $\dfrac{\sqrt{70p}}{49p}$
    (D) $\dfrac{2\sqrt{3p}}{21p}$

Simplify the below to the lowest positive terms.

7. $$\dfrac{4\sqrt{7a^2b^4}}{\sqrt{8ab}}$$

(A) $26\sqrt{6ab}$

(B) $\dfrac{4b\sqrt{35ab}}{5}$

(C) $b\sqrt{14ab}$

(D) $2b\sqrt{3ab}$

Solve the below inequalities.

1. $-7x - 5(x - 1) \leq 89$

   (A) No solution   (B) $x \geq -10$ (C) $x \geq -7$ (D) $x \geq -6$

2. $123 > -3 + 6(1 - 5x)$

   (A) $x > -4$ (B) $x > -23$ (C) $x > -34$ (D) $x > -5$

3. $5(5x - 3) + 8 < -132$

   (A) $x < -39$ (B) $x < -10$ (C) $x < -5$ (D) $x < -35$

4. $282 < -6 - 8(-1 + 5k)$

   (A) No solution   (B) {All real numbers}   (C) $k < -37$ (D) $k < -7$

5. $7(x - 7) \leq -84$

   (A) $x \leq -12$ (B) $x \leq -5$ (C) $x \leq -40$ (D) $x \leq -28$

6. $87 \leq -4(-6 + 2r) - r$

   (A) $r \geq -2$ (B) $r \leq -7$ (C) $r \leq -16$ (D) $r \geq -16$

7. $-84 \geq 7(-6 + 1k)$

   (A) $k \leq 2$ (B) No solution   (C) $k \leq -6$ (D) $k \leq -27$

8. $-105 < -5(1 - 5p)$

   (A) $p > -8$ (B) $p > -22$ (C) $p > -24$ (D) $p > -4$

One-step word problems #18

1. Dan was 70 years old when I visited him 9 years ago. How old is he now?

   (A) 79   (B) 61   (C) 75   (D) 88

2. How old is Jason if he was 75 years old thirteen years ago?

   (A) 62   (B) 101   (C) 100   (D) 88

3. Sam spent $42 on soda packs. If they cost $6 / pack, how many packs did he buy?

   (A) 7   (B) 12   (C) 11   (D) 10

4. If the weight of a package is multiplied by $\frac{3}{4}$ the result is 61.2 lbs. Find the weight of the package.

   (A) 81.6   (B) 61.1   (C) 70.2   (D) 57.4

5. A recipe for pancakes calls for 7 cups of flour. Lucy accidentally put in 10 cups. How many extra cups did she put in?

   (A) 5   (B) 2   (C) 1   (D) 3

6. Mason and his best friend got a cash prize. They divided the money evenly, each getting $26. How much money was the cash prize ?

(A) $48　　　(B) $52　　　(C) $42　　　(D) $13

7. Julia and her friends ate 20 muffins. If they ate $\frac{5}{8}$ of what they had originally. How many muffins were there ?

(A) 36　　　(B) 32　　　(C) 12.5　　　(D) 34

Circles #19

1. Find the area of the circle given diameter = 4 m.

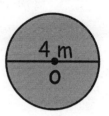

(A) 12π m^2 (B) 9π m^2
(C) 7π m^2 (D) 4π m^2

2. Find the area of the circle given diameter = 10 m.

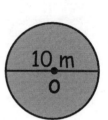

(A) 25π m^2 (B) 50π m^2
(C) 42π m^2 (D) 34π m^2

3. Find the area of the circle given diameter = 6 in.

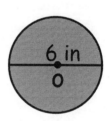

(A) 4π in^2 (B) 12π in^2
(C) 16π in^2 (D) 9π in^2

4. Find the area of the circle given diameter = 24 ft.

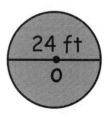

(A) 1296π ft^2 (B) 144π ft^2
(C) 36π ft^2 (D) 9π ft^2

5. Find the area of the circle given diameter = 12 in

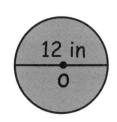

(A) 36π in^2 (B) 62π in^2
(C) 44π in^2 (D) 52π in^2

6. Find the area of the circle given diameter = 22 yd.

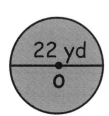

(A) 64π yd^2 (B) 16π yd^2
(C) 121π yd^2 (D) 22π yd^2

7. Find the area of the circle given diameter = 14 km.

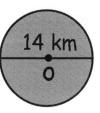

(A) 64π km^2 (B) 8π km^2
(C) 49π km^2 (D) 59π km^2

8. Find the area of the circle given diameter = 8 ft.

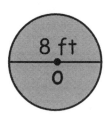

(A) 22π ft^2 (B) 9π ft^2
(C) 16π ft^2 (D) 6π ft^2

1. Find the volume of the sphere with a radius of 13.2 mi and round the answer to the nearest tenth.

(A) 9634.1 mi³ (B) 5587.7 mi³

(C) 6705.2 mi³ (D) 4817 mi³

2. Find the volume of the sphere with a diameter of 13.6 mi and round the answer to the nearest tenth.

(A) 2370.8 mi³ (B) 1185.4 mi³

(C) 2679 mi³ (D) 1317.1 mi³

3. Find the volume of the sphere with a diameter of 12.6 m and round the answer to the nearest tenth.

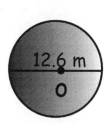

(A) 1149.9 m³ (B) 1047.4 m³

(C) 999.9 m³ (D) 900.8 mi³

4. Find the volume of the sphere with a radius of 12 ft and round the answer to the nearest tenth.

(A) 7238.2 ft³ (B) 4620.9 ft³

(C) 3619.1 ft³ (D) 4125.8 ft³

**QUANT Q
GEOMETRIC FIGURES
Vol 1**

**Volume
Sphere
#20**

5. Find the volume of the sphere with a diameter of 24.6 mi and round the answer to the nearest tenth.

(A) 5827.4 mi³ (B) 5244.7 mi³
(C) 7794.8 mi³ (D) 6547.6 mi³

6. Find the volume of the sphere with a diameter of 2.2 ft and round the answer to the nearest tenth.

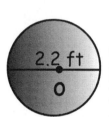

(A) 6.5 ft³   (B) 13 ft³
(C) 11.4 ft³ (D) 5.6 ft³

7. Find the volume of the sphere with a diameter of 2.1 cm and round the answer to the nearest tenth.

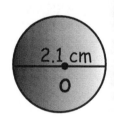

(A) 3.05 cm³ (B) 3.88 cm³
(C) 3.5 cm³   (D) 4.84 cm³

8. Find the volume of the sphere with a radius of 17.2 cm and round the answer to the nearest tenth.

(A) 21314.5 cm³ (B) 23659.1 cm³
(C) 42628.9 cm³ (D) 21314.4 cm³

©All rights reserved-Math-Knots LLC., VA-USA
For more practice visit www.a4ace.com

**QUANT Q
GEOMETRIC FIGURES
Vol 1**

Volume rectangle
Square prisms
#21

1. Find the volume of the rectangular prism measuring 1 ft and 4 ft along the base and 2 ft tall. Round the answer to the nearest tenth.

   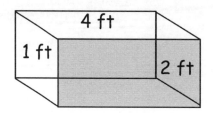

   (A) 8 ft^3 (B) 4 ft^3

   (C) 9.2 ft^3 (D) 4.6 ft^3

2. Find the volume of the rectangular prism measuring 15 in. and 18 in. along the base and 15 in. tall. Round the answer to the nearest tenth.

   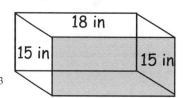

   (A) 3361.5 in^3 (B) 2689.2 in^3

   (C) 3173.3 in^3 (D) 4050 in^3

3. Find the volume of a square prism measuring 3 yd along each edge of the base and 17 yd tall. Round the answer to the nearest tenth.

   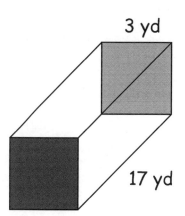

   (A) 128.5 yd^3 (B) 153 yd^3

   (C) 115.8 yd^3 (D) 131.6 yd^3

4. Find the volume of a rectangular prism measuring 11 ft and 3 ft along the base and 7 ft tall. Round the answer to the nearest tenth.

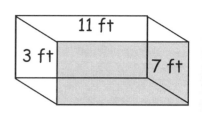

(A) 924 ft^3 (B) 462 ft^3

(C) 1848 ft^3 (D) 231 ft^3

5. Find the volume of a square prism measuring 17 km along each edge of the base and 19 km tall. Round the answer to the nearest tenth.

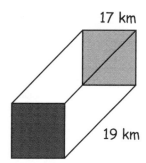

(A) 4101.8 km^3 (B) 5491 km^3

(C) 3363.5 km^3 (D) 4557.5 km^3

6. Find the volume of a square prism measuring 10 cm along each edge of the base and 7 cm tall. Round the answer to the nearest tenth.

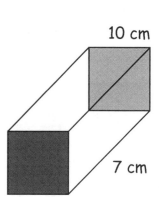

(A) 1416.2 cm^3 (B) 833 cm^3

(C) 708.1 cm^3 (D) 700 cm^3

7. Find the volume of a square prism measuring 12 in. along each edge of the base and 14 in. tall. Round the answer to the nearest tenth.

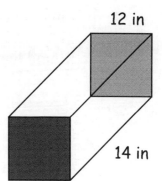

(A) 2016 in³   (B) 4032 in³

(C) 4636.8 in³ (D) 2318.4 in³

8. Find the volume of a rectangular prism measuring 18 m and 7 m along the base and 16 m tall. Round the answer to the nearest tenth.

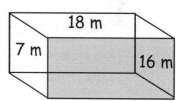

(A) 2016 m³   (B) 4032 m³

(C) 1633 m³   (D) 1453.4 m³

1. Find the volume of a cylinder with a diameter of 34 ft and a height of 12 ft.
   Round the answer to the nearest tenth.

   (A) 21598.4 ft^3 (B) 10895 ft^3
   (C) 21790.1 ft^3 (D) 18303.7 ft^3

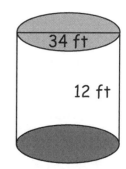

2. Find the volume of a cylinder with a radius of 6 mm and a height of 6 mm.
   Round the answer to the nearest tenth.

   (A) 678.6 mm^3 (B) 3013 mm^3
   (C) 1357.2 mm^3 (D) 2714.4 mm^3

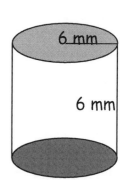

3. Find the volume of a cylinder with a diameter of 22 in and a height of 15 in.
   Round the answer to the nearest tenth.

   (A) 2394.9 in^3 (B) 4789.7 in^3
   (C) 5702 in^3 (D) 1197.5 in^3

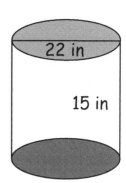

4. Find the volume of a cone with a diameter of 8 m and a height of 10 m.
Round the answer to the nearest tenth.

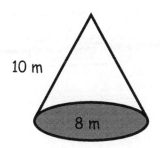

(A) 335.1 m³   (B) 402.1 m³

(C) 167.6 m³   (D) 804.2 m³

5. Find the volume of a cone with a radius of 3 km and a height of 10 km.
Round the answer to the nearest tenth.

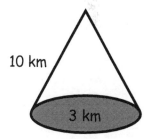

(A) 108.4 km³   (B) 94.2 km³

(C) 98.9 km³   (D) 119.2 km³

6. Find the volume of a cylinder with a radius of 14 yd and a height of 9 yd.
Round the answer to the nearest tenth.

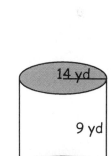

(A) 5541.8 yd³   (B) 4876.8 yd³

(C) 2770.9 yd³   (D) 2438.4 yd³

7. Find the volume of a cone with a diameter of 4 in and a height of 15 in.
Round the answer to the nearest tenth.

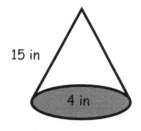

(A) 43.8 in³   (B) 55.9 in³

(C) 62.8 in³   (D) 49.8 in³

Find the value of x for the below questions.

1)
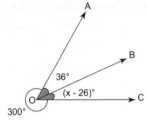

A) 48 B) 40
C) 50 D) 46

2)
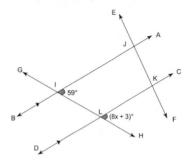

A) 16 B) 9
C) 12 D) 7

3)
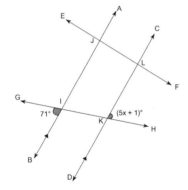

A) -1 B) 0
C) 14 D) 7

4)
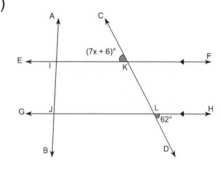

A) 14 B) 13
C) 8   D) 5

5)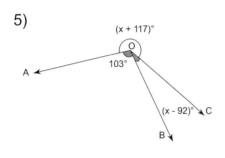

A) 122 B) 118
C) 115 D) 116

6)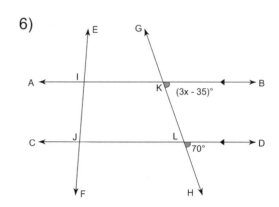

A) 35 B) 33
C) 31 D) 30

7)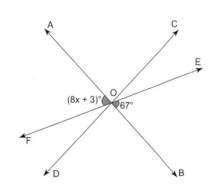

A) 7   B) 8
C) 15 D) 9

8)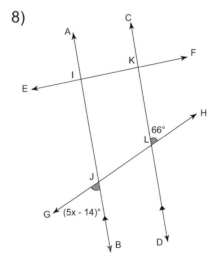

A) 16 B) 13
C) 21 D) 14

Find the measure of the ∠x for the below questions:

1)

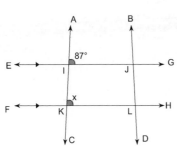

A) 155° B) 87°
C) 93°   D) 3°

2)

A) 130° B) 67°
C) 50°   D) 113°

3)

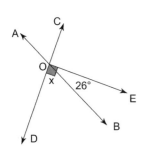

A) 93°   B) 154°
C) 26°   D) 64°

4)

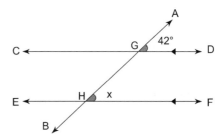

A) 42°   B) 132°
C) 138° D) 48°

5)

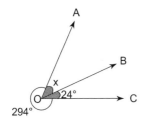

A) 42°   B) 132°
C) 48°   D) 138°

6)

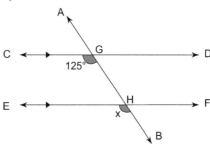

A) 145° B) 35°
C) 125° D) 55°

7)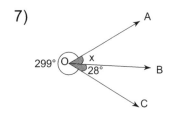

A) 57°   B) 147°
C) 33°   D) 123°

8)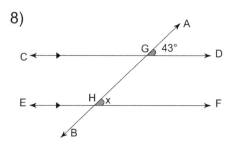

A) 146°   B) 43°
C) 137°   D) 56°

Describe the transformation and find the transformation rule.

1)
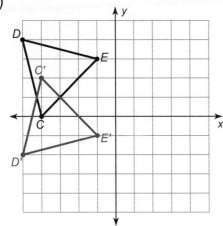

A) Reflection across $y = 1$
B) Reflection across $x = -1$
C) Reflection across $y = -1$
D) Reflection across the x-axis

2)
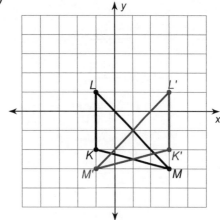

A) Reflection across $x = -2$
B) Reflection across $y = -1$
C) Reflection across $y = 1$
D) Reflection across $x = 1$

3)
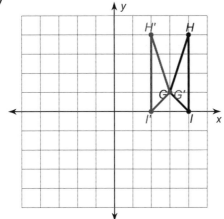

A) Reflection across $x = 1$
B) Reflection across $x = -3$
C) Reflection across $x = -1$
D) Reflection across $x = 3$

4)
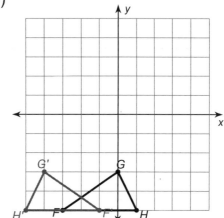

A) Rreflection across the y-axis
B) Reflection across $x = -2$
C) Reflection across $y = -2$
D) Reflection across $y = 1$

Reflection #25

Describe the transformation and find the transformation rule.

5)
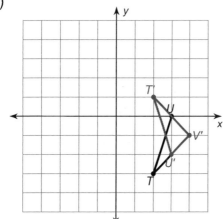

A) Reflection across y = 1
B) Reflection across the y-axis
C) Reflection across x = -1
D) Reflection across y = -1

6)
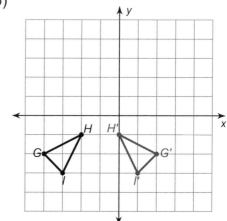

A) Reflection across x = -1
B) Reflection across the y-axis
C) Reflection across x = 1
D) Reflection across y = -1

7)
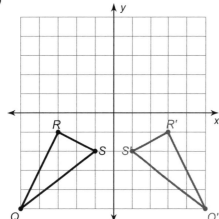

A) Reflection across x = 1
B) Reflection across the y-axis
C) Reflection across y = -1
D) Reflection across x = 2

8)
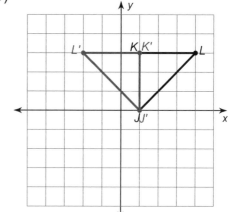

A) Reflection across the x-axis
B) Reflection across y = 2
C) Reflection across x = 1
D) Reflection across x = -1

Describe the transformation and find the transformation rule.

1)
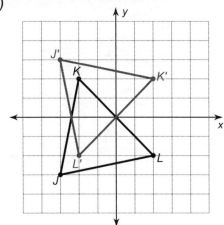

A) Rotation 180° counterclockwise about the origin
B) Translation: 1 unit right and 1 unit up
C) Rotation 90° clockwise about the origin
D) Rotation 270° about the origin

2)
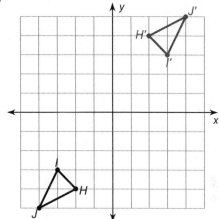

A) Rotation 180° counterclockwise about the origin
B) Rotation 180° about the origin
C) Translation: 8 units right and 5 units up
D) Rotation 90° clockwise about the origin

3)
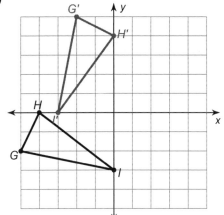

A) Rotation 90° clockwise about the origin
B) Reflection across y = 4
C) Rotation 180° counterclockwise about the origin
D) Rotation 90° about the origin

4)
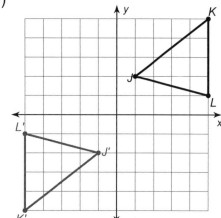

A) Rotation 90° clockwise about the origin
B) Translation: 4 units left
C) Translation: 2 units left
D) Rotation 180° about the origin

Describe the transformation and find the transformation rule.

5)

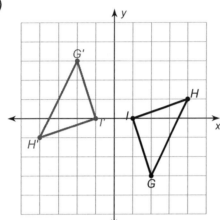

A) Rotation 90° counterclockwise
B) Rotation 180° about the origin
C) Reflection across the y-axis
D) Rotation 90° clockwise about the origin

6)

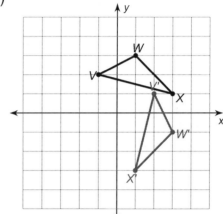

A) Rotation 180° counterclockwise about the origin
B) Translation: 3 units left and 4 units up
C) Rotation 90° clockwise about the origin
D) Rotation 180° about the origin

7)

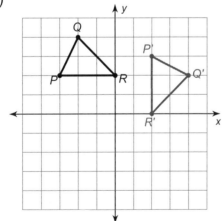

A) Rotation 270° about the origin
B) Rotation 90° clockwise about the origin
C) Rotation 180° counterclockwise about the origin
D) Reflection across $y = 5$

8)

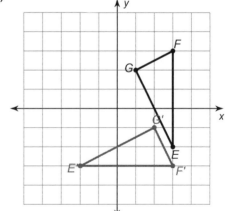

A) Rotation 180° counterclockwise about the origin
B) Translation: 5 units left and 3 units up
C) Rotation 90° clockwise about the origin
D) Rotation 270° about the origin

Translation #27

Write a rule to describe each transformation.

1)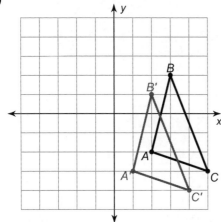

A) Translation: 4 units left and 3 units up
B) Translation: 1 unit left and 1 unit down
C) Translation: 1 unit left and 2 units up
D) Translation: 3 units left and 2 units up

2)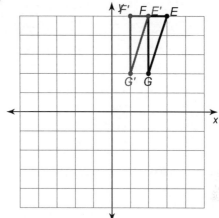

A) Translation: 2 units left and 2 units down
B) Translation: 1 unit right and 1 unit down
C) Translation: 1 unit left
D) Translation: 1 unit right and 2 units down

3)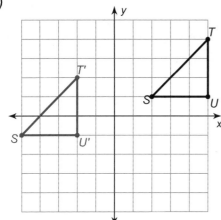

A) Translation: 7 units left
B) Translation: 7 units left and 2 units down
C) Translation: 4 units left and 2 units down
D) Translation: 4 units left and 4 units down

4)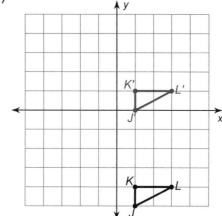

A) Translation: 5 units left and 1 unit down
B) Translation: 5 units up
C) Translation: 2 units left and 3 units up
D) Translation: 1 unit right and 6 units up

5)
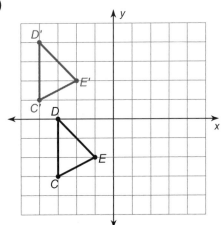

A) Translation: 1 unit left and 4 units up
B) Translation: 4 units right
C) Translation: 1 unit left and 4 units down
D) Translation: 2 units right and 4 units up

6)
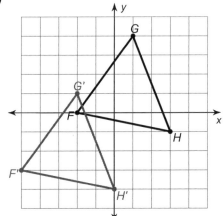

A) Translation: 3 units left and 3 units down
B) Translation: 4 units left and 3 units down
C) Translation: 3 units up
D) Translation: 3 units right

7)
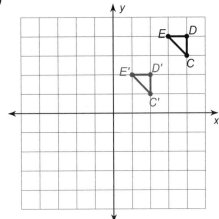

A) Translation: 5 units left and 2 units down
B) Translation: 4 units left and 2 units up
C) Translation: 2 units left and 1 unit down
D) Translation: 2 units left and 2 units down

8)
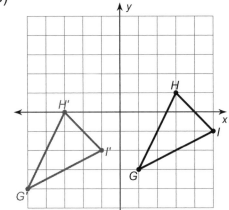

A) Translation: 6 units left and 1 unit up
B) Translation: 1 unit left and 5 units down
C) Translation: 6 units left and 1 unit down
D) Translation: 5 units right

Quant Q
TJHSST

Practice Test - 1

Warm up 1

1. Evaluate $m(p + (-2)^3 + q)$; where $m = -4$, $p = -10$, and $q = 2$

   (A) 69 (B) 63
   (C) 64 (D) 56

2. Evaluate $|7 - 7m| = 63$, and find the sum of the solutions.

   (A) 2   (B) -8
   (C) 80 (D) 18

3. If $\left(\frac{1}{4}\right)^{-k} = 16^{2k+3}$, $k^2 - 2k =$

   (A) 12 (B) -8
   (C) 0   (D) 8

4. Find $x + y$ if $x - y = 6$ and $3x - 13y = 208$.

   (A) -32 (B) -21
   (C) -6   (D) 17

5. A straight line of slope $\frac{5}{2}$ is passing through the points $A(x, -2)$ and $B(1, 3)$. Find the value of x.

   (A) 6   (B) -1
   (C) -7 (D) 7

6. A parallelogram has a base of 24 inches and height of 15 inches. Find its area.

   (A) 36 in²   (B) 3.6 in²
   (C) 3600 in² (D) 360 in²

7. If $R \# P = R + P - 1$, then what is the value of

   $1 \# (2 \# 3)$?

   (A) 8   (B) 4
   (C) 11 (D) 16

8. The below box and whisker plots summarize the math test scores of grade 8 and grade 7

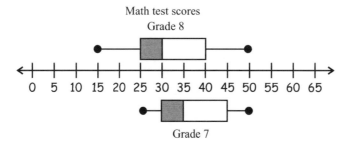

Based on the above data, which of the below statements is true ?

(A) The least score of grade 7 students is 15
(B) The highest score of grade 8 students is 45
(C) The least score of grade 8 students is 15
(D) No grade 7 students got a score of 50

9. Rik got 91, 91, 97, 94 and 95 on the math test. What is his average math score ?

(A) 93.6 (B) 93
(C) 94.5 (D) 92.6

10. Rak reads a book of 350 pages. How many 5's are there in page numbers ?

(A) 61 (B) 66
(C) 55 (D) 64

11. ZipZing company is selling their hand bags for $175 which were originally priced as $250. What is the percentage of the discount offered ?

(A) 40% (B) 80%
(C) 75% (D) 30%

12. Rak puts her hand in a pile of 7 red beads, 8 green beads, and 5 gold beads. What is the probability that she chooses a red bead ?

(A) $\frac{7}{20}$ (B) $\frac{1}{4}$

(C) $\frac{8}{20}$ (D) $\frac{1}{5}$

13. If the length of the Square K is doubled, then its perimeter increases by ?

    (A) 4 (B) 2
    (C) 8 (D) 16

14. Pat can build a doll house in 12 hours. Lucy can build the same doll house in 16 hours. Together they can complete to build a doll house in how many hours ?

    (A) 6.86 (B) 6.76
    (C) 6.80 (D) 6.87

15. When you reverse digits in a certain two digit number you increase its value by 27. What is the number if the sum of its digits is 5 ?

    (A) 23 (B) 19
    (C) 17 (D) 14

Practice Test 1

1. In a garden, there are 10 rows and 12 columns of Apple trees. The distance between any two trees is 2 meters and a distance of one meter is left from all sides of the boundary of the garden. The length of the garden is

   (A) 20 m   (B) 22 m

   (C) 24 m   (D) 26 m

2. The compound interest for principle X is $1025 for 2 years and the simple interest on same principle is $1000. With the same rate of interest and number of years, What will be the principle amount for a simple interest of $1500 ?

   (A) $2500   (B) $3500

   (C) $3750   (D) $4000

3. The perimeter of a rectangular field is thrice the perimeter of a square field. If one of the sides of the square field is 24 m and breadth of the rectangular field is 48 m then find the area of the rectangular field ?

   (A) 4276 Sq.m   (B) 5354 Sq.m

   (C) 3892 Sq.m   (D) 4608 Sq.m

4. Olivia bought a bag for $36.75, which was originally priced at $52.50. Find the discount offered by the store ?

   (A) 60%   (B) 30%

   (C) 40%   (D) 15%

5. Lydia sold a hand bag for $32.19. She purchased the bag at $22.99 . Find her profit percentage ?

   (A) 20%   (B) 9%

   (C) 40%   (D) 10%

6. Claire is purchasing a land priced at $16,500 and she pays a tax of 5%.
   Find the selling price of the land.

   (A) $17,325.00   (B) $14,025.00

   (C) $13,200.00   (D) $18,150.00

7. Dan added 18 instead of 13.6 in his calculation. Find the percentage change in his calculation

   (A) 24.4% increase   (B) 4.4% decrease

   (C) 132.4% increase   (D) 32.4% increase

Quant Q TJHSST — Practice Test - 1

8. A farmhouse shelters 14 animals. Some are horses and some are geese. Altogether there are 48 legs. How many geese are there in the farmhouse?

   (A) 12 geese (B) 4 geese
   (C) 10 geese (D) 11 geese

9. Sam took a loan of $53,300 at 6% interest compounded semi annually for 8 years. Find the amount he needs to pay at the end of the loan term.

   (A) $85,530.85 (B) $135,400.74
   (C) $84,952.10 (D) $78,884.00

10. Find the missing terms in the below arithmetic sequences.

    ..., -10, ___, ___, ___, 14, ...

    (A) -9, -14, -19 (B) 2, 8, 14
    (C) -10, -16, -22 (D) -4, 2, 8

11. Find the missing terms in the below arithmetic sequences.

    ..., 8, ___, ___, ___, ___, ___, 1208, ...

    (A) -192, -392, -592, -792, -992
    (B) 208, 408, 608, 808, 1008
    (C) -392, -592, -792, -992, -1192,
    (D) -592, -792, -992, -1192, -1392

12. Find the missing terms in the below sequences.

    ..., 2, ___, 8, ...

    (A) 12 (B) 6
    (C) -12 (D) 4

13. Write the explicit formula for the below number series.
    1, -4, 16, -64, 256, ...

14. How many lb of brand X coffee which costs $25/lb must be added to 14 lb of brand Y coffee which costs $10/lb to make Rak's special coffee blend which costs $11/lb?

   (A)   3 lbs
   (B)   4 lbs
   (C)   6 lbs
   (D)   1 lb

15. Shan went to drop his daughter at the train station and came back home. The trip there took five hours and the trip back took four hours. What was Shan's average speed on the trip if he averaged 60 km/h on the return trip?

   (A)   30 km/h
   (B)   20 km/h
   (B)   50 km/h
   (D)   48 km/h

16. If $P(B) = \dfrac{13}{20}$ $P(A \text{ and } B) = \dfrac{143}{400}$ then $P(A) = $?

   (A) $\dfrac{11}{80}$
   (B) $\dfrac{11}{20}$
   (C) $\dfrac{63}{400}$
   (D) $\dfrac{1}{20}$

17. Henry flipped a coin three times and then rolls a fair six-sided dice five times. Find the probability of the coin showing heads-up every time and the dice showing an even number every time.

   (A) $\dfrac{28}{121}$
   (B) $\dfrac{1}{256}$
   (C) $\dfrac{8}{165}$
   (D) $\dfrac{10}{273}$

18. A magic bag has eight nickels and seven dimes. Rak picks a coin from the bag and gives it her brother Rik. She picks another coin and gives it to him as well. Find the probability that the first coin is a nickel and the second coin is a dime.

   (A) $\dfrac{1}{36}$
   (B) $\dfrac{1}{8}$
   (C) $\dfrac{1}{27}$
   (D) $\dfrac{4}{15}$

19. Working together, Rik and Rak can harvest a field in 8.06 hours. Had she done it alone it would have taken Rak 19 hours. How long would it take Rik to do it alone?

   (A)   13.69 hours
   (B)   13.99 hours
   (C)   15 hours
   (D)   16.02 hours

20. Two pipes P and Q can fill the tank within 12 hours and 18 hours respectively. Pipe R can empty the tank in 36 hrs. If all three pipes are opened, find the time taken to fill the tank?

    (A) 8 hours   (B) 9 hours
    (C) 10hours   (D) 12 hours

21. A cube is painted with red, black and green colors. Opposite faces are painted with same color. How many small cubes are there where one face is green and other one is either black or red ?

    (A) 28   (B) 8
    (C) 16   (D) 24

22. For the given series below

    $$-4, -2, 0, \ldots$$

    If $\begin{cases} a(1) = A \\ a(n) = a(n-1) + B \\ A = ?, B = ? \end{cases}$, find $A^2 + B^2$

    (A) 20   (B) 2
    (C) 4   (D) 36

23. Danny has a 6 sided dice. marked by number four on four sides and number two is marked on the remaining two sides. Which statement best describes Danny's chance of winning the game by getting the number 4?

    (A) Certainly will win   (B) Certainly will lose
    (C) Most likely will win   (D) Most likely will lose

24. The formula for blood flow rate is given by $F = \dfrac{P_1 - P_2}{r}$

    where F is the flow rate, P_1 the initial pressure, P_2 the final pressure and r the resistance created by blood vessel size. Which formula can not be derived from the given formula ?

    (A) $P_1 = Fr + P_2$ (B) $P_2 = P_1 - Fr$
    (C) $r = F(P_2 - P_1)$ (D) $r = \dfrac{P_1 - P_2}{F}$

25. A box contains 10 red beads, 12 gold beads, 15 black beads, 13 green beads. Chuck picks bead from the box, what is the probability that it will be a gold or a black bead?

(A) 54 % (B) 43 %
(C) 59 % (D) 68 %

26. The parallel side of a trapezium are 29 inches and 11 inches and non parallel side of length 13 inches and 15 inches. Find the distance between the parallel sides.

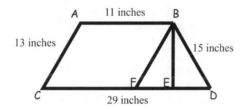

(A) 15 inches (B) 11 inches
(C) 12 inches (D) 14 inches

27. In a string of beads for every 2 gold beads there are 3 green beads. What is the color of 223rd bead?

(A) Gold (B) Green
(C) Blue (D) None

28. Sam took a loan of $205 at 12% interest for 7 years. Find the amount he needs to pay at the end of the loan term.

(A) $377.20 (B) $453.19
(C) $248.19 (D) $229.60

Warm up 2

1. Evaluate $p(1 - m) - \dfrac{m}{4}$; where m = 4, and p = 7

   (A) −22 (B) −31
   (C) −17 (D) −27

2. Find the sum of the solutions of |x − 6| = 5

   (A) 6 (B) $\dfrac{9}{5}$
   (C) $\dfrac{-5}{3}$ (D) 12

3. If $3^{-2x} \cdot 3^{x+1} = \dfrac{1}{81}$, find the value of $x^2 + 1$

   (A) $-\dfrac{1}{8}$ (B) 26
   (C) 6 (D) $\dfrac{25}{9}$

4. Find $x^2 + y^2$ if x + y = −6 and 11x − y = 18

   (A) 50 (B) 17
   (C) 53 (D) 28

5. A straight line of slope $-\dfrac{1}{2}$ is passing through the points $A(-9, -2)$ and $B(x, -9)$. Find the value of x.

   (A) -2 (B) 1
   (C) 5 (D) -5

6. Simplify a - (a² + bc) ; where a = 3 , b = -15 and c = 5

   (A) 61 (B) 78
   (C) 58 (D) 69

7. Hazel purchased a book at $6.95 and sells it for 35% price increase. Find the selling price of the book ?

   (A) $4.52 (B) $9.38
   (C) $2.43 (D) $6.60

8. Working alone it takes Beth 15 hours to harvest a field. Mei can harvest the same field in 9 hours. Find how long it would take them if they worked together ?

   (A)   4.3 hours   (B)   7.15 hours

   (C)   5.63 hours   (D)   5.82 hours

9. Jason is preparing to bake a new year cake. Her recipe needs $5\frac{1}{9}$ cups of sugar. Instead she adds $5\frac{5}{6}$ cups of sugar. How many extra cups of sugar did she add ?

   (A) $5\frac{1}{9}$ (B) $5\frac{1}{6}$

   (C) $10\frac{17}{18}$ (D) $\frac{13}{18}$

10. Find the volume of a cylinder with a radius of 10 cm and a height of 16 cm. Answer to the nearest tenth

    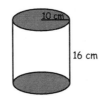

    (A)   3096.7 cm³   (B)   5026.5 cm³

    (C)   2789.8 cm³   (D)   2513.3 cm³

11. Which of the below options form a right angle triangle ?

    (A)   28 cm , 45 cm , 46 cm   (B)   39 cm , 80 cm , 81 cm

    (C)   32 cm , 60 cm , 68 cm   (D)   30 cm , 40 cm , 41 cm

12. Fix Nut company charges $25.65 for fixing the air in car tyres, which was originally priced at $28.50. What is the percentage of the discount ?

    (A)   30%   (B)   20%

    (C)   15%   (D)   10%

13. If we toss a coin 4 times, how many different outcomes are possible ?

    (A)   8   (B)   10

    (C)   16   (D)   12

14. Which of the below options describes the transformation of the below figure GEF ?

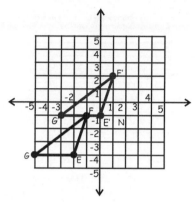

(A)   reflection across y = -1

(B)   translation of 2 units right and 3 units up

(C)   rotation of 90° clockwise about the origin

(D)   translation of 5 units right and 1 unit down

15. The below box and whisker plots summerize the science quiz scores of grade 8 and grade 7

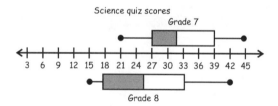

Based on the above data , which of the below statements is true ?

(A)   The least score of grade 8 students is 21
(B)   The highest score of grade 8 students is 55
(C)   The highest score of grade 7 students is 45
(D)   The least score of grade 7 students is 15

Practice Test 2

1. Maria, Bina and Cathy entered into a partnership with investment of $ 24000, $ 32000 and $ 48000 respectively. After one year Maria withdrew $4000 and Bina invested $8000 more. And after one more year Maria invested $15000 more and Cathy withdrew $8000. At the end of three years, they earned a profit of $114450. Find the share of Maria in the total profit?

   (A) $33500 (B) $30250
   (C) $27650 (D) $35750

2. Zack rows from shore A to B which is at a distance of 120 km and come back in 8 hours. He can row 20 km with the stream in the same time as 12 km against the stream. The rate of the stream is?

   (A) 12 km/hr (B) 16 km/hr
   (C) 10 km/hr (D) 8 km/hr

3. Jackson sells two types of candles. He sells small candles for $12 and big candles for $14. He can only sell a maximum of 40 candles per week. "m" represents the number of small candles and "g" represents the number of big candles. If he needs to earn at least $250 this week, which system of inequalities represents the given conditions?

   (A) m + g <= 40 / 12m + 14g >= 250
   (B) m + g >= 250 / 12m + 14g <= 40
   (C) m + g <= 250 / 12m + 14g >= 40
   (D) m + g <= 40 / 12m + 14g <= 250

4. A box contains 8 puzzles, 4 dictionaries, 3 story books, 10 magazines Rosy picks an item from the box, what is the probability that it will be a puzzle or a story book?

   (A) 30 % (B) 39 %
   (C) 22 % (D) 44 %

5. Find the approximate length of the missing side AC from the below figure

   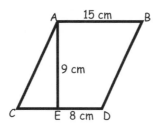

   (A) 12 cm (B) 15 cm
   (C) 11 cm (D) 21 cm

6. The parallel side of a trapezium are 35 inches and 19 inches and non parallel side of length 17 inches and 17 inches. Find the distance between the parallel sides.

   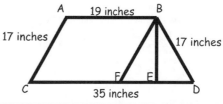

   (A) 15 inches (B) 27 inches
   (C) 24 inches (D) 13 inches

7. In a class, 20% of the members own only two cars each, 40% of the remaining own three cars each and the remaining members own only one car each. Find the percentage of members having one car?

   (A) 52% (B) 48%
   (C) 60% (D) 80%

8. In an election between two contestants, 20 % of the voters didn't vote and 160 votes are declared invalid. The winner gets 39 % of the votes and declared win by 310 votes. Then find the number of voters in the voting list?

   (A) 6000 (B) 4500
   (C) 6250 (D) 6500

9. Robert purchased a X - Box at $629.99 and sells it at a 55% price increase. Find the selling price of the X - Box.

   (A) $566.99 (B) $346.49
   (C) $283.50 (D) $976.48

10. Find the sum of the series as given below
    $a_1 = 8$, $a_n = 36$, n = 15

    (A) 337 (B) 333
    (C) 660 (D) 330

11. Rak added number 4 instead of 95 in her calculation. Find the percentage change in her calculations.

    (A) 94.8% increase (B) 95.8% decrease
    (C) 132.4% increase (D) 32.4% increase

12. Beth took a loan of $460 at 10% interest for 9 years. Find the amount she needs to pay at the end of the loan term

    (A) $506.00 (B) $1,084.66
    (C) $414.00 (D) $874.00

13. Jack took a loan of $26,000 at 6% interest compounded semi annually for 8 years. Find the amount he needs to pay at the end of the loan term.

    (A) $35,692.43 (B) $30,463.14
    (C) $30,487.04 (D) $30,160.00

Practice Test - 2

14. A farmhouse shelters 14 animals. Some are horses and some are geese. Altogether there are 48 legs. How many horses are there in the farmhouse ?

   (A) 4 horses (B) 10 horses
   (C) 2 horses (D) 3 horses

15. Find the missing terms in the below arithmetic sequences

   ..., 36, ___, ___, 636, ...

   (A) 236, 436 (B) 239, 439
   (C) 238, 438 (D) 439, 639

16. Find the missing terms in the below sequences

   ..., -5, ___, ___, ___, ___, ___, 49, ...

   (A) 4, 13, 22, 31, 40 (B) 3, 11, 19, 27, 35
   (C) 12, 21, 30, 39, 48 (D) 3, 12, 21, 30, 39

17. Find the missing terms in the below sequences

   ..., -4, ___, -16, ...

   (A) -8, (B) -6
   (C) -2 (D) -4

18. Write the explicit formula for the below number series
   1 , 1, , 2, , ...

19. How many lbs of almonds which cost $6/lb must be added to 3 lbs of cashews which cost $11/lbs to make mixed nuts which cost $9/lb?

   (A) 3 lbs (B) 5 lbs
   (C) 6 lbs (D) 2 lbs

20. Working together, Dan and Ron can build a bird house in 7.17 hours. Had he done it alone it would have taken Ron 13 hours. How long would it take for Dan to complete the work ?

   (A) 12.32 hours (B) 15.99 hours
   (C) 12.96 hours (D) 18.43 hours

Quant Q TJHSST

Practice Test - 2

21. A private jet made a round trip from Virginia to New york. It took eight hours to reach and the trip back took ten hours. If the jet averaged 46 km/h faster to reach than on the return trip. Find the private jet's average speed on the outbound trip.

    (A) 335 km/h (B) 320 km/h
    (C) 110 km/h (D) 230 km/h

22. If $P(B) = \dfrac{3}{5}$ $P(A|B) = \dfrac{3}{8}$ then $P(A \text{ and } B) = ?$

    A) $\dfrac{143}{400}$ (B) $\dfrac{9}{40}$
    C) $\dfrac{11}{20}$ (D) $\dfrac{3}{20}$

23. Rita flips a coin five times and then rolls a fair six-sided dice once. Find the probability of the coin landing heads-up every time and the dice showing a four

    (A) $\dfrac{1}{27}$ (B) $\dfrac{1}{1024}$
    (C) $\dfrac{28}{135}$ (D) $\dfrac{1}{192}$

24. There are five boys and five girls in a class. The teacher randomly selects three different students to answer questions. Find the probability of choosing the first student a boy, the second student is a girl, and the third student a girl.

    (A) $\dfrac{5}{36}$ (B) $\dfrac{1}{28}$
    (C) $\dfrac{10}{39}$ (D) $\dfrac{1}{4}$

25. 5 years ago Rita and Geetha's ages are in the ratio of 5:6 and 5 years hence the ratio of their ages becomes 6:7. Find the current age of Geetha ?

    (A) 60 (B) 65
    (C) 70 (D) 55

26. Find the volume of the cylinder whose radius is 2 times of breadth of rectangle whose perimeter is 90 cm, and length and breadth is in the ratio of 2:1 and cylinder height is equal side of square whose diagonal value is $20\sqrt{2}$ cm ?

    (A) 47852 cm^3 (B) 26871 cm^3
    (C) 56571 cm^3 (D) 69879 cm^3

27. Find $f(3)$ if $f(x) = f(x-1) + 2.x^2$ and we know that $f(1) = -2$

   (A) 6   (B) 24

   (C) 30   (D) 18

28. Raksha's average score on the two Social tests is 94. If she wants to get an average score of 95 in three tests of this quarter, what should be her score in the third test ?

   (A) 89   (B) 95

   (C) 90   (D) 97

Warm up 3

1. Evaluate $|n + 6| = 1$, And find the sum of the solutions

   (A) 12 (B) -2

   (C) -12 (D) -10

2. Find $x + y^2$ if $15x + 19y = 95$ and $2x - 19y = 228$

   (A) 114 (B) 119

   (C) 206 (D) 86

3. A straight line of slope $\dfrac{7}{9}$ is passing through the points $A(-4, -6)$ and $B(x, 1)$. Find the value of x.

   (A) 6 (B) 4

   (C) -4 (D) 5

4. Find the equation of the straight line perpendicular to $y = \dfrac{3}{2}x - 5$ and passing through the point $C(-2, 4)$

   (A) $y = -\dfrac{5}{3}x + \dfrac{8}{3}$ (B) $y = -\dfrac{2}{3}x + \dfrac{8}{3}$

   (C) $y = \dfrac{2}{3}x + \dfrac{8}{3}$ (D) $y = \dfrac{5}{3}x + \dfrac{8}{3}$

5. The original price of a microscope is $624.50. If the discount offered on the microscope is 35%, what would be its selling price?

   (A) $686.95 (B) $218.57

   (C) $405.93 (D) $562.05

6. Volume(V) of the rectangular box DEFG is 64 cubic ft, with length equals to 8 ft and width as 2 ft. what is the height of the rectangular box DEFG?

   (A) 1 (B) 6

   (C) 3 (D) 4

Practice Test - 3

7. Solve for U and T. If U + T = 29 and UT = 100 where U and T are positive integers.

   (A) 25 and 2 (B) 14 and 15

   (C) 25 and 4 (D) 20 and 9

8. If R # P = 2R + P - 5 what is the value of $\dfrac{2 \# 3}{1 \# 2} = \boxed{?}$

   (A) 4 (B) 2

   (C) -2 (D) 1

9. Rik is running a race that is K miles long. If he has completed 17 miles distance. Which expression below shows the number of miles remaining to finish the race ?

   (A) K + 17 (B) K - 17

   (C) K × 17 (D) $\dfrac{K}{17}$

10. Dan mows the lawn in ten hours. Tom can mow the same lawn in 15 hours. Together they can complete to mow the same lawn in how many hours.

    (A) 5 hours (B) 4 hours

    (C) 7 hours (D) 6 hours

11. A straight line passes through the points (-2, -2) and (0, p) with slope as $\dfrac{9}{2}$ then p = ?

    (A) 7 (B) 5

    (C) -7 (D) 1

12. When 5% of tax is added to a milk can of $10.00. What is the sale price.

    (A) $10.50 (B) $0.50

    (C) $9.50 (D) $11.50

13. Maria had a coupon of 50% discount. She selected a dress priced at $15.96. What will be the selling price of the dress after discount.

    (A) $23.92 (B) $18.34

    (C) $7.90 (D) $7.98

14. Evaluate $_{24}C_4 - 1$

    (A) 255,023   (B) 255,024

    (C) 2,125   (D) 10,625

15. Evaluate $\dfrac{^{10}P_{10}}{5}$

    (A) 670,580   (B) 90,720

    (C) 525,430   (D) 725,760

Practice Test 3

1. The radius of the circular ground is 24m and area of inner circle $616 m^2$. Find the width of circular track?

   (A) 10 m (B) 12 m

   (C) 15 m (D) 9 m

2. A train of length 120 meters, is moving at a speed of 30 m/s can, crosses a platform of x meters long in 20s. What is the length of the platform?

   (A) 520 m (B) 420 m

   (C) 480 m (D) 410 m

3. Rita says, "If you reverse my own age, the figures represent my friend Amy's age. she is, of course, senior to me and the difference between our ages is one-eleventh of their sum." Find Rita's age?

   (A) 23 years (B) 34 years

   (C) 45 years (D) 30 years

4. David gets on the elevator at the 11th floor of a building and rides up at the rate of 57 floors per minute. At the same time, Albert gets on an elevator at the 51st floor of the same building and rides down at the rate of 63 floors per minute. If they continue travelling at these rates, then at which floor will their paths cross?

   (A) 19 (B) 28

   (C) 30 (D) 37

5. Cathy purchased a Play Station at $219.99 and sells it at a 20% price increase. Find the selling price of the Play Station.

   (A) $175.99 (B) $252.99

   (C) $230.99 (D) $263.99

6. Dora added 60 instead of 33 in her calculations. Find the percentage change in her calculations.

   (A) 81.8% decrease (B) 27% increase

   (C) 81.8% increase (D) 98.4% increase

7. Andy gave a personal loan to Tim an amount of $365 at 10% interest. If Tim repays it after 4 years, how much amount did Andy received?

   (A) $36.50 (B) $534.40

   (C) $511.00 (D) $146.00

Practice Test - 3

8. Find the missing terms in the below arithmetic sequences

   ..., 27, ___, ___, ___, 827, ...

   (A) -171, -369, -567   (B) 227, 427, 627
   (C) -173, -373, -573   (D) -172, -371, -570

9. Find the missing terms in the below sequences

   ..., -2, ___, ___, ___, ___, ___, 1198, ...

   (A) 197, 396, 595, 794, 993   (B) -203, -402, -601, -800, -999
   (C) 195, 394, 593, 792, 991   (D) 198, 398, 598, 798, 998

10. Find the missing terms in the below sequences

    ..., -3, ___, -48, ...

    (A) 4   (B) -12
    (C) 1   (D) -8

11. Write the explicit formula for the below number series

    2, 5, 10, 17, 26, ...

12. Bella mixes together 5 gallons of Brand X fruit juice and 4 gallons of apple juice. Find the percentage of fruit juice in Brand X if the mixture contains 50% fruit juice.

    (A) 16%   (B) 10%
    (C) 6%   (D) 5%

13. Working alone, John can solve a puzzle in 15 minutes. One day he worked with his friend Henry and it only took 6.67 minutes to solve the puzzle. How long does it take Henry to solve the puzzle by himself?

    (A) 9.86 minutes   (B) 12.01 minutes
    (C) 15.46 minutes   (D) 14.92 minutes

14. Maya made a trip to her grandparents house and back. The trip there took four hours and the trip back took five hours. She averaged 24 mi/h on the return trip. Find her average speed to reach her grandparents house ?

    (A) 40 mi/h (B) 45 mi/h
    (C) 30 mi/h (D) 35 mi/h

15. $P(A) = \dfrac{9}{20}$ $P(A \text{ and } B) = \dfrac{27}{80}$ then $P(B) = ?$

    (A) $\dfrac{1}{4}$ (B) $\dfrac{9}{20}$
    (C) $\dfrac{3}{4}$ (D) $\dfrac{1}{5}$

16. A bag contains four red marbles, five blue marbles, and three yellow marbles. Three times, you randomly pick a marble, return it to the bag, and then mix the marbles. Find the probability of picking the first marble as red, the second marble as blue, and the third marble as yellow.

    (A) $\dfrac{1}{4}$ (B) $\dfrac{2}{9}$
    (C) $\dfrac{5}{18}$ (D) $\dfrac{5}{144}$

17. Rik has four white socks, six brown socks, and six black socks. Find the probability of him randomly picking two matching pair of black socks ?

    (A) 0.045 (B) 0.044
    (C) 0.125 (D) 0.255

18. The difference between simple interest and compound interest on $35000 at the rate of 12 % per annum for 2 years is?

    (A) $ 782 (B) $504
    (C) $656   (D) $958

19. Tanya sold her book rack at a loss of 13 %. If she had sold the book rack for $ 84 more, he would have gained 15%. Find the selling price of the book rack to get a profit of 20 %?

    (A) $360 (B) $420
    (C) $ 480 (D) $ 500

Quant Q TJHSST

Practice Test - 3

20. Jack reads a book of 140 pages. How many 3's are there in page numbers?

    (A) 29   (B) 31

    (C) 27   (D) 34

21. A minute cell divides into 3 parts every 3 minutes. In 30 minutes how many cells are formed?

    (A) 3^9 (B) 3^{10}

    (C) 3^{15} (D) 30

22. Sai runs at the rate of 5 miles per half hour. Sam runs at the rate of 1.5 times faster than his friend sai. If sams speed is Y miles per hour. What is the value of Y?

    (A) 7.5 miles per hour   (B) 15 miles per hour

    (C) 7.5 miles   (D) 12 miles per hour

23. Maria and Kate are selling baked goods for a school fundraiser. They are selling cupcakes and sugar cookies. Mary sold 7 cupcakes and 12 sugar cookies for total $162. Jasmine sold 10 cupcakes and 6 sugar cookies for total $120. Find the cost a cupcake and a sugar cookie.

    (A) cupcake = $6, sugar cookie = $10
    (B) cupcake = $2, sugar cookie = $10
    (C) cupcake = $6, sugar cookie = $5
    (D) cupcake = $10, sugar cookie = $8

24. How many unique permutations of the letters in the word **DOUBLES** are possible?

    (A) 5040   (B) 5620

    (C) 6020   (D) 3840

25. 100 people attended a local charity event. If each of the attendies shake hands with everyone else how many hand shakes are done?

    (A) 990   (B) 4920

    (C) 3650   (D) 4950

26. Amy gave a personal loan to Sara an amount of $1,700 at 4% interest, compounded annually. If Sara repays it after 3 years, how much amount will Amy receive?

    (A) $1,904.00   (B) $1,912.27

    (C) $1,919.26   (D) $1,905.06

27. There are 15 animals in the barn. Some are chickens and some are sheep. There are 50 legs in all. How many of each animal are there ? How many chickens are there in the barn ?

    (A)　　5 chickens　　　　　　　　　　(B)　　12 chickens

    (C)　　13 chickens　　　　　　　　　 (D)　　11 chickens

28. Two machines X and Y takes 2 inputs and produce one output which is greatest of all. Outputs of machines X and Y become inputs to machine Z and the greatest of all becomes the output. Based on the given information and the below figure what is the final output produced ?

    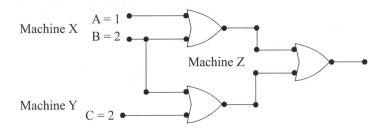

    (A)　　1　　　　　　　　　　　　　　(B)　　4
    (C)　　3　　　　　　　　　　　　　　(D)　　2

Warm up 4

1. Evaluate $y(y + y + z + 3)$; where $y = 7$, and $z = -8$

   (A) 55 (B) 63

   (C) 70 (D) 69

2. Evaluate $|-6 + 7m| = 50$, and find the sum of the solutions

   (A) $\frac{1}{2}$ (B) 8

   (C) $\frac{11}{3}$ (D) $\frac{12}{17}$

3. If $36 \cdot 6^{-3r-1} = 6^{-2r}$, find the value of $r^2 + 5r$?

   (A) -4 (B) 2

   (C) 6 (D) 5

4. Find $(x + y)^2$ if $4x + 17y = 119$ and $26x + 17y = -255$

   (A) 18 (B) 36

   (C) 34 (D) 289

5. A straight line of slope $-\frac{1}{5}$ is passing through the points $A(-8, 9)$ and $B(7, y)$. Find the value of y.

   (A) 9 (B) 8

   (C) -2 (D) 6

6. Find the equation of the straight line perpendicular to $y = -\frac{2}{7}x + 4$ and passing through the point D(3, 4)

   (A) $y = \frac{7}{2}x - \frac{13}{2}$ (B) $y = \frac{13}{2}x + \frac{7}{2}$

   (C) $y = x + \frac{7}{2}$ (D) $y = -\frac{13}{2}x + \frac{7}{2}$

7. Brand X of a vacuum cleaner is sold at a price of $109.95. A store is offering a 40% discount today. Find the selling price of the vacuum cleaner.

    (A) $131.94 (B) $93.46

    (C) $65.97   (D) $43.98

8. Find the volume of a square prism measuring 7 ft along each edge of the base and 8 ft tall. Answer to the nearest tenth

    (A) 392 ft³   (B) 593.4 ft³

    (C) 345 ft³   (D) 690 ft³

9. Which of the below options form a right angle triangle ?

    (A) 21 , 28 , 34   (B) 14 , 48 , 49

    (C) 39 , 80 , 87   (D) 12 , 35 , 37

10. Which of the below options describes the transformation of the below figure XYZ ?

    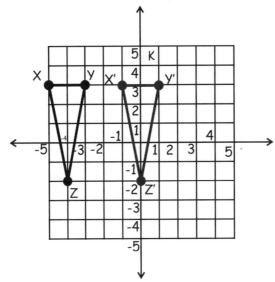

    (A) translation of 6 units to right and 2 units up

    (B) translation of 2 units right and 1 unit up

    (C) rotation across x = -2

    (D) translation of 4 units right

11. Find the volume of a cone with a diameter of 16 cm and a height of 20 cm.
Answer to the nearest tenth.

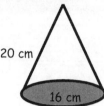

(A) 1340.4 cm³ (B) 1139.4 cm³

(C) 649.5 cm³ (D) 569.7 cm³

12. Monopoly game costs $25.00. The store is offering a discount of 30% on it. What is the selling price of the game?

(A) $26.25 (B) $7.50

(C) $32.50 (D) $17.50

13. Evaluate $\dfrac{^{11}P_6}{9} = ?$

(A) 30,640 (B) 32,924

(C) 36,960 (D) 33,241

14. Working alone, Jack pick forty bushels of apples in 11 hours. Julia can pick the same amount in 9 hours. Find how long it would take them if they worked together.

(A) 4.45 hours (B) 5.9 hours

(C) 3.89 hours (D) 4.95 hours

15. Evaluate $\dfrac{^{13}C_7}{11} = ?$

(A) 128 (B) 844

(C) 240 (D) 156

Practice Test 4

1. A monkey climbs 30 feet at the beginning of each hour and rests for a while and slips back 20 feet. He starts back again at the beginning of the next hour. If he starts climbing at 8.00 a.m., at what time will he reach 120 feet from the ground?

   (A) 4 p.m. (B) 5 p.m.
   (C) 6 p.m. (D) 3 a.m

2. Diameter of a circle is 3/5th of sum of length and breadth of rectangle. The perimeter of rectangles is 60 m and length of rectangle is 1.5 times of breath of rectangle. Find the area of circle?

   (A) 306.5 m^2 (B) 216.5 m^2
   (C) 254.5 m^2 (D) 297.5 m^2

3. Find the number of unique permutations of the word **EQUINOX** can be formed ?

   (A) 7,540 (B) 4,280
   (C) 6,120 (D) 5,040

4. Kim purchased a Monopoly game for $19.95 and sold at 90% price hike. What is the selling price of the monopoly game ?

   (A) $17.95 (B) $37.91
   (C) $37.80 (D) $1.99

5. The original price of a car is $37,000.00 and the tax need to be paid for the car is 6%, what is the selling price of the car ?

   (A) $2,220.00 (B) $39,220.00
   (C) $34,780.00 (D) $42,550.00

6. Ella added 66 in her calculations instead of 81.7. Find the percentage change in her calculations.

   (A) 23.8% increase (B) 19.2% decrease
   (C) 15.7% increase (D) 80.8% decrease

7. Lola gave a personal loan to Rosy an amount of $1,330 at 6% interest. If Rosy repays it after 8 years, how much amount did Lola received ?

   (A) $2,119.82 (B) $1,968.40
   (C) $1,409.80 (D) $638.40

Practice Test - 4

8. Find the missing terms in the below arithmetic sequences

..., 29, ___, ___, 23, ...

(A) 25, 23 (B) 21, 18
(C) 27, 25 (D) 24, 21

9. Find the missing terms in the below sequences

..., -35, ___, ___, ___, ___, ___, -65, ...

(A) -30, -27, -24, -21, -18 (B) -32, -29, -26, -23, -20
(C) -40, -45, -50, -55, -60 (D) -30, -25, -20, -15, -10

10. Find the missing terms in the below sequences

..., 2, ___, ___, 16, ...

(A) 16, 32 (B) 4, 2
(C) 4, 8 (D) 8, 16

11. Write the explicit formula for the below number series

33, 39, 45, 51, 57, ...

12. Liam mixes 8 L of Brand A fruit juice and 4 L of Brand B fruit juice which contains 38% orange juice. Find the percent of orange juice in Brand A if the mixture contained 36% orange juice.

(A) 55% (B) 35%
(C) 19% (D) 10%

13. Working alone, Ella can build a bird cage in 15 hours. One day her friend Rocky helped her and it only took 8.57 hours. How long does it take Rocky to build it alone?

(A) 19.99 hours (B) 15.23 hours
(C) 14.93 hours (D) 16.34 hours

14. If $P(B) = \dfrac{2}{5}$ $P(A \text{ and } B) = \dfrac{3}{25}$ then $P(A) = ?$

    (A) $\dfrac{7}{10}$ (B) $\dfrac{77}{400}$

    (C) $\dfrac{7}{20}$ (D) $\dfrac{3}{10}$

15. There are six nickels and six dimes in your pocket. Three times, you randomly pick a coin out of your pocket, return it to your pocket, and then mix-up the change in your pocket. All three times, the coin is a nickel.

    (A) $\dfrac{3}{11}$ (B) $\dfrac{24}{91}$

    (C) $\dfrac{1}{8}$ (D) $\dfrac{36}{1331}$

16. Marked Price of a furniture set gives 30% of profit in its cost price. if store gives 10%, 15% successive discount on the furniture set, and it is sold for $1989. Find the selling price of the furniture set if he sells at 115% of original cost price?

    (A) $ 1750 (B) $ 2250

    (C) $ 2000 (D) $ 2300

17. Two machines X and Y takes 2 inputs and produce one output which is greatest of all. The outputs of machines X and Y become inputs to machine Z and get added to produce the output. Based on the given information and the below figure find the missing input value B ?

    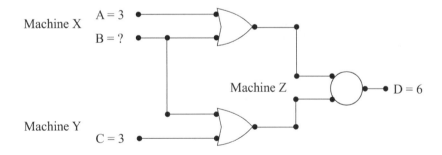

    (A) 6 (B) 3

    (C) 2 (D) Cannot be determined

18. A box contains 11 Skittles, 4 Sneakers, 10 Twigs, 12 Kit-Kats, 13 M & M's. Harper picks an item from the box, what is the probability that it would be a M & M or a Kit-Kat ?

    (A) 25 % (B) 50 %

    (C) 75 % (D) 55 %

Practice Test - 4

19. Tom completes his walking on circular ground X by 36 minutes and Mary completes her walking on another circular ground Y by 90 minutes. The total length of Ground X is 3/5 times of the total length of Ground Y. Find the speed ratio of Mary to Tom ?

(A) 2:3   (B) 3:2

(C) 4:1   (D) 1:4

20. Find the missing letter from the below series

A , H , F , M , K , R , P , ?

(A) D   (B) W

(C) L   (D) X

21. The base of a triangular sign board is 23 feet with a height of 17 feet. Find the cost of painting it at the rate of $2 per square feet.

(A) $391   (B) $195.5

(C) $198   (D) $401

22. From a square sheet of side 14 inches a circular sheet with maximum dimensions is taken away. Find the area of the remaining sheet.

(Note : $\Pi = \frac{22}{7}$)

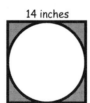

(A) 154 in^2 (B) 196 in^2

(C) 64 in^2 (D) 42 in^2

23. How many unique permutations of the letters in the word **SPECTRUM** can be formed ?

(A) 40,220   (B) 40,320

(C) 38,450   (D) 42,580

24. When the integer *n* is divided by 17, the quotient is x and the reminder is 5. When *n* is divided by 23, the quotient is x and the reminder is 14. Which of the following is true ?

(A) 23x + 17y = 19   (B) 17x - 23y = 9

(C) 17x + 23y = 19   (D) 14x + 5y = 6

Quant Q TJHSST — Practice Test - 4

25. Ken gave a personal loan to Ben an amount of $5,800 at 8% interest. compounded annually. If Ben repays it after 6 years, how much amount will Ken receive ?

   (A) $8,584.00 (B) $9,203.87

   (C) $9,214.91 (D) $9,189.22

26. There are 15 animals in the barn. Some are chickens and some are sheep. There are 50 legs in all. How many of each animal are there ? How many sheeps are there in the barn ?

   (A) 10 sheeps (B) 3 sheeps

   (C) 2 sheeps (D) 4 sheeps

27. Ship X left Port A and traveled to reach Port B. Ship Y left eight hours later traveling 12 mph faster in an effort to catch up to it. After six hours Ship Y speed is caught up to Ship X. What was the average speed of Ship X ?

   (A) 13 mph (B) 11 mph

   (C) 8 mph (D) 9 mph

28. There are six boys and four girls in a class. The teacher randomly selects three different students to answer questions. Find the probability of teacher choosing the first student a boy, the second and third students as girls.

   (A) 0.1 (B) 0.074

   (C) 0.25 (D) 0.048

Warm up 5

1. Evaluate $|6m - 7| = 43$, and find the sum of the solutions.

   (A) $2\frac{1}{3}$ (B) $\frac{2}{5}$

   (C) $\frac{1}{2}$ (D) $\frac{25}{3}$

2. If $3^k \cdot 3^{-35} = 3^{2k}$ then $2k + 100 = ?$

   (A) 70   (B) 30

   (C) -35   (D) -70

3. Find $(x - y)^2$ if $7x + 19y = -285$ and $15x - 19y = -133$

   (A) -1   (B) -15

   (C) 11   (D) 121

4. A straight line of slope $\frac{7}{3}$ is passing through the points $A(-5, 4)$ and $B(x, -3)$. Find the value of x.

   (A) 2   (B) 5

   (C) -9   (D) -8

5. Find the equation of the straight line perpendicular to $y = -4$ and passing through the point $E(-5, -5)$

   (A) $y = 5$ (B) $x = -5$

   (C) $x = 5$ (D) $y = \frac{5}{3}$

6. Maria purchased a dining table set for $64.95. Find out the selling price if 2% tax is added to the purchase of the dining table?

   (A) $61.70   (B) $63.65

   (C) $1.30   (D) $66.25

7. A cell phone cover has two flaps side. One flap is of the length 8.92×10^{-6} and the other is 1.60×10^{-6}. What is the difference in the lengths of flaps?

   (A) 7.32×10^{-6} (B) 0.732×10^{-6}

   (C) 0.0732×10^{-6} (D) 73.2×10^{-6}

8. The function f(y) = 35 + 15 h represents the amount of money, in dollars. where h is the no of hours Shan worked. He works 10 hours this week. How much money did he earn this week ?

   (A)   165

   (B)   225

   (C)   185

   (D)   180

9. Which of the below graph best represents the function

   $$f(x) = x^2 + 5x + 4$$

   (A)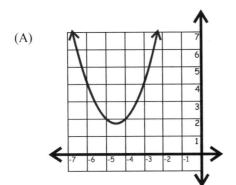

   (B)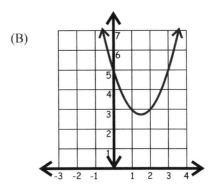

   (C)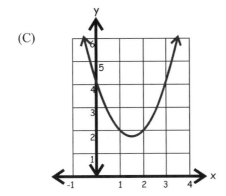

   (D)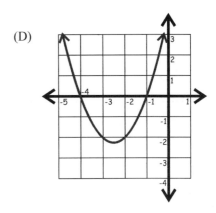

10. Dora solved puzzles each day over spring break. The number of puzzles she solved in seven days is shown.

    13 , 11 , 13 , 15 , 10 , 13 , 9

    She then solved 15 more puzzles on last day. How are the mean and median affected ?

    (A)   The mean increased and the median remained the same.

    (B)   The median increased and the mean remained the same.

    (C)   The median and the mean both remained the same.

    (D)   The mean and the median both decreased.

11. Find the sum of the below matrices ?

$$\begin{vmatrix} 5 & 7 \\ -2 & -4 \\ 1 & 6 \end{vmatrix} + \begin{vmatrix} 11 & 9 \\ 15 & 8 \\ 3 & -1 \end{vmatrix}$$

(A) $\begin{vmatrix} 15 & -5 \\ 10 & 20 \\ -3 & -1 \end{vmatrix}$

(B) $\begin{vmatrix} 16 & 16 \\ 13 & 4 \\ 4 & 5 \end{vmatrix}$

(C) $\begin{vmatrix} 7 & 17 \\ -8 & 9 \\ 5 & -4 \end{vmatrix}$

(D) $\begin{vmatrix} 10 & -12 \\ 16 & -6 \\ 2 & -11 \end{vmatrix}$

12. Evaluate the below matrices

$$\begin{vmatrix} -6 & 1 \\ 4 & 3 \\ 0 & 5 \end{vmatrix} - \begin{vmatrix} 9 & 3 \\ -2 & 0 \\ 3 & 1 \end{vmatrix} = ?$$

(A) $\begin{vmatrix} 15 & 8 \\ 5 & 4 \\ 9 & 7 \end{vmatrix}$

(B) $\begin{vmatrix} -15 & -2 \\ 6 & 3 \\ -3 & 4 \end{vmatrix}$

(C) $\begin{vmatrix} 14 & 7 \\ 2 & -13 \\ 15 & -21 \end{vmatrix}$

(D) $\begin{vmatrix} -9 & 15 \\ 7 & 17 \\ 15 & -1 \end{vmatrix}$

13. The function f(y) = (5/3) m, represents the amount of muffins baked by Beth. Where m is the number of muffins she gave to her friends. If she shares 24 muffins with her friends, How many muffins did she make originally ?

   (A) 44   (B) 38

   (C) 25   (D) 40

14. If the thickness of a pile of 80 card boards is 117.20 mm (milli meters), how many card boards will there be in a pile which is 703.20 mm thick ?

   (A) 488   (B) 480

   (C) 670   (D) 467

15. Find the average of all the prime numbers between 30 and 50 ?

   (A) 39.8   (B) 42

   (C) 35.5   (D) 29.4

Practice Test 5

1. An Intercity bus charges are comprised of a fixed charge, together with the charge of the distance covered. For a journey of 16 miles, the charges paid are $15.6 and for a journey of 24 miles, the charges paid are $20.4. What will a person have to pay for traveling a distance of 30 miles ?

   (A) $ 20 (B) $ 24
   (C) $ 48 (D) $ 12

2. Mary makes a profit of $1 on the first day at her new stores. On every subsequent day, she earns an income which is just double of the previous day. One the 10th day of business, her income is

   (A) $ 2^9 (B) $ 2^{10}
   (C) $18 (D) $ 102

3. Mia wants to go to concert and the tickets are priced at $184.50. Her friend gave her a coupon of 35% on the concert tickets. How much does the ticket costs after the discount ?

   (A) $119.93 (B) $166.05
   (C) $118.92 (D) $64.58

4. Bryan purchased an Apartment at $54,000.00 and sells it at a 40% price hike. Find the selling price of the Apartment.

   (A) $21,600.00 (B) $62,100.00
   (C) $75,600.00 (D) $27,000.00

5. Stella added 63 in her accounts instead of 82. What is the percentage change ?

   (A) 19% decrease (B) 30.2% increase
   (C) 19% increase (D) 23.2% decrease

6. Henry took a loan of $1,320 at 12% interest for 2 years. Find the amount he needs to pay at the end of the loan term.

   (A) $1,478.40 (B) $1,636.80
   (C) $316.80 (D) $1,655.81

7. A farmhouse shelters 23 animals. Some are pigs and some are chickens. Altogether there are 84 legs. How many of each animal are there ? How many chickens are there in farmhouse ?

   (A) 4 chickens (B) 20 chickens
   (C) 21 chickens (D) 8 chickens

Quant Q TJHSST

Practice Test - 5

8. Find the missing terms in the below arithmetic sequences

..., -31, ___, ___, -58, ...

(A) -22, -13 (B) -24, -15
(C) -23, -13 (D) -40, -49

9. Find the missing terms in the below sequences

..., 22, ___, ___, ___, ___, ___, 82, ...

(A) 30, 40, 50, 60, 70 (B) 8, -4, -16, -28, -40
(C) 32, 44, 56, 68, 80 (D) 32, 42, 52, 62, 72

10. Find the missing terms in the below sequences

..., 1, ___, 36, ...

(A) $-\dfrac{7}{3}$ (B) 6
(C) 1 (D) $-\dfrac{1}{3}$

11. Write the explicit formula for the below number series

$2, 2, \dfrac{8}{3}, 4, \dfrac{32}{5}, ...$

12. Ben wants to make 14 oz. of alloy containing 83% copper. He is planning on melting and combine metal X containing 89% copper with metal Y containing 75% copper. How much quantity of metal X and metal Y are needed to create alloy ?

(A) 8 oz. of 89% copper, 6 oz. of 75% copper
(B) 4 oz. of 89% copper, 10 oz. of 75% copper
(C) 5 oz. of 89% copper, 9 oz. of 75% copper
(D) 10 oz. of 89% copper, 4 oz. of 75% copper

13. Cathy can water the plants in 15 minutes. Macy can do the same in 11 minutes How long will it take them if they worked together ?

(A) 6.32 minutes (B) 6.79 minutes
(C) 6.35 minutes (D) 5 minutes

Quant Q TJHSST

Practice Test - 5

14. A train X left Virginia and traveled to Newyork . Another train Y left one hour later traveling 7 km/h faster in an effort to catch up to train X. After ten hours train Y is finally caught up. Find the average speed of train X ?

    (A) 70 km/h
    (B) 40 km/h
    (C) 90 km/h
    (D) 120 km/h

15. A vending machine contains thirteen bottles of sports drinks : four lemon-lime flavored, four orange flavored, and five fruit-punch flavored. Three times, Andy randomly grabs a bottle, return the bottle to the cooler, and then mix up the bottles. Find the probability of him picking up the first time, a lemon-lime drink. The second and third times, a fruit-punch.

    (A) $\dfrac{1}{20}$
    (B) $\dfrac{1}{4}$
    (C) $\dfrac{1}{12}$
    (D) $\dfrac{100}{2197}$

16. If $P(A) = \dfrac{3}{5}$, $P(B) = \dfrac{9}{20}$ then $P(A \text{ and } B) = ?$

    (A) $\dfrac{27}{80}$
    (B) $\dfrac{27}{100}$
    (C) $\dfrac{27}{200}$
    (D) $\dfrac{7}{80}$

17. There are seven nickels and six dimes in Zara's bag. She randomly picks a coin from her bag and gives it to her sister. She randomly picks another coin and give it off. Find the probability that the first coin is a nickle and second is a dime ?

    (A) $\dfrac{1}{4}$
    (B) $\dfrac{1}{192}$
    (C) $\dfrac{1}{128}$
    (D) $\dfrac{7}{26}$

18. A printer numbers the pages of a story book starts with 1 and uses 3189 digits in all. How many pages does the book have?

    (A) 1000
    (B) 1074
    (C) 1075
    (D) 1080

19. Dan and John's salaries are in the ratio 8: 9 and their expenditures are in the ratio of 33: 37. If Dan saves $ 14000 and John saves $ 16000, then find the income of Dan?

    (A) $ 35000
    (B) $ 50000
    (C) $ 80000
    (D) $ 60000

Practice Test - 5

20. A handbag was sold at a discount of 25 % and there was a profit of 20 %. If the profit earned was $ 100 less than the discount offered, then find the selling price of the handbag ?

   (A) $ 650
   (B) $ 700
   (C) $ 750
   (D) $ 600

21. The table below shows math test scores of grade 7 students

   75 , 62 , 70 , 60 , 62

   Miss Rosy, the math teacher missed to add students score. If the median and mode of the data is same. what is the missing score ?

   (A) 62
   (B) 55
   (C) 75
   (D) 60

22. Find the number of terms in the arithmetic series given below

   $a_1 = -5$, $a_n = -75$, $s_n = -600$

   (A) 19
   (B) 16
   (C) 13
   (D) 15

23. Find the number of terms in the series given below

   $$\sum_{i=1}^{n} (6i - 13) = 525$$

   (A) 16
   (B) 15
   (C) 18
   (D) 11

24. Find the number of terms in the series given below

   $$\sum_{i=1}^{7} \left(\frac{-1}{3}\right)^{i-1}$$

   (A) $\frac{547}{729}$
   (B) $\frac{547}{726}$
   (C) $\frac{547}{728}$
   (D) $\frac{3}{4}$

25. Find the number of terms in the below series

$$a_1 = 2, r = -5, s_n = 42$$

(A) 7 (B) 5

(C) 6 (D) 3

26. In how many unique ways the letters of the word **BRIGHTLY** be arranged ?

(A) 40,320 (B) 38,470

(C) 28,320 (D) 40,240

27. The figure below shows the dimensions of isosceles triangle in terms of x. Find the area of the triangle ?

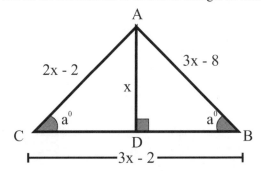

(A) 24 (B) 30

(C) 48 (D) 60

28. Two machines X and Y takes 2 inputs and produce one output which is product of all. Based on the given information and the below figure find the missing value ?

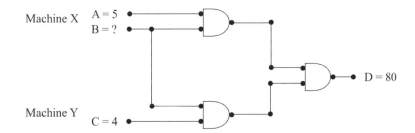

(A) 10 (B) 2

(C) 4 (D) 20

Warm up 6

Evaluate the below expressions.

1. Evaluate $h - h + 4 + j^2$; where $h = -3$, and $j = 7$

    (A) 49 (B) 53
    (C) 59 (D) 46

2. Evaluate $|-7x - 9| = 16$, and find the sum of the solutions.

    (A) $\dfrac{18}{7}$ (B) $\dfrac{9}{2}$
    (C) $\dfrac{-7}{3}$ (D) $\dfrac{-18}{7}$

3. If $64^{-p+2} \cdot 16 = 16$

    (A) -10 (B) -2
    (C) 6 (D) 2

4. Find $x + y^2$ if $16x - 13y = -143$ and $3x + 13y = -104$

    (A) 25 (B) 38
    (C) -12 (D) 12

5. A straight line of slope $-\dfrac{5}{6}$ is passing through the points $A(-7, 6)$ and $B(5, y)$. Find the value of x.

    (A) -9 (B) -4
    (C) -2 (D) 2

6. A shop is offering 20% discount for one day on a video game that is priced at $9.99? What is the selling price of the video game after discount?

    (A) $6.10 (B) $7.99
    (C) $7.68 (D) $7.20

7. Evaluate $\dfrac{^{21}C_4}{3} = ?$

    (A) 1654 (B) 1125
    (C) 1490 (D) 1995

8. The original price of a chocolate bar is $2.20 and a 1% sales tax is added to the price. Find the sale price of the chocolate bar ?

(A) $2.10 (B) $2.90
(C) $0.22 (D) $2.22

9. Evaluate $-3 + {}^{25}C_3$

(A) 3,841 (B) 2,297
(C) 2,043 (D) 4,112

10. Evaluate $5 + {}^{18}P_5$

(A) 1028165 (B) 1128160
(C) 153165   (D) 958165

11. John bought 2 adult tickets and one child ticket at Fairfax carnival for $30.50. Lucy bought 3 adult tickets and one child ticket at Fairfax carnival for $40.40. What is the price of the adult ticket ?

(A) $10.45 (B) $8.90
(C) $9.90   (D) $6.10

12. Jack has the rope of length 205.8073×10^{-2}. He needs a rope of length 2172.67×10^{-3}. How much more rope does he need to buy ?

(A) 114.596×10^{-6} (B) 114.597×10^{-6}
(C) 114.597×10^{-3} (D) 1145.975×10^{-3}

13. If 8 ft long iron rod of uniform thickness weighs 28 lb, what will be the weight of 10 ft long iron rod of the same thickness ?

(A) 34.8 (B) 35.9
(C) 35   (D) 36

14. The sum of two numbers is 30 and their difference is eight. Find the product of the numbers ?

(A) 209 (B) 201
(C) 309 (D) 219

15. Which of the below graph best represents the function

$$f(x) = x^2 + 9x + 18$$

(A)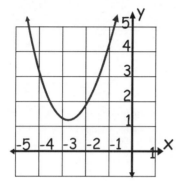

(B)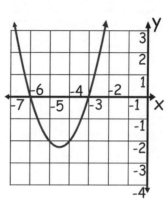

(C)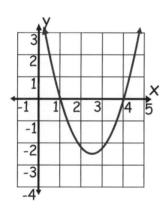

(D)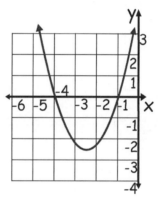

Practice test 6

1. Three colored boxes Red, Green and Blue, together have 108 balls. There are twice as many balls in the green and red boxes combined as there are in the blue box and twice as many in the blue box as there are in the red box. How many balls are there in the green box ?

   (A)   18   (B)   36

   (C)   45   (D)   54

2. A number consists of two digits whose sum is 11. If 27 is added to the number, then the digits change their places. Find the number ?

   (A)   47   (B)   65

   (C)   83   (D)   92

3. Roma purchased a Furniture set at $8,400.00 and sells it at a 80% price increase. What is the selling price of the Furniture set ?

   (A) $15,120.00   (B) $7,980.00

   (C) $6,720.00   (D) $1,680.00

4. The circumference of a circle is half of the perimeter of a rectangle. The area of circle is 1386 sq.m. What is the area of the rectangle if 50 m is its width ?

   (A)   4100 sq.m   (B)   4353 sq.m

   (C)   3600 sq.m   (D)   4900 sq.m

5. Find the percentage change from 76 cm to 12 cm.

   (A)   15.8% decrease   (B)   133.3% increase

   (C)   69.5% decrease   (D)   84.2% decrease

6. Jade took a loan of $21,100 at 14% interest for 2 years. Find the amount she needs to pay at the end of the loan term.

   (A) $27,026.39   (B) $27,008.00

   (B) $24,054.00   (D) $27,421.56

7. John took a loan of $870 at 4% interest compounded semi annually for 5 years. Find the amount he needs to pay at the end of the loan term.

   (A) $1,060.53   (B) $1,044.00

   (C) $1,287.81   (D) $1,058.49

8. A farmhouse shelters 23 animals. Some are pigs and some are chickens. Altogether there are 84 legs. How many of each animal are there ? How many pigs are there in farmhouse ?

   (A) 19 pigs   (B) 2 pigs
   (C) 2 pigs   (D) 3 pigs

9. Find the missing terms in the below sequences

   ..., -5, ___, ___, -23, ...

   (A) -11, -17   (B) -6, -9
   (C) -8, -13   (D) -10, -15

10. Find the missing terms in the below sequences

    ..., -23, ___, ___, ___, ___, ___, 577, ...

    (A) 75, 173, 271, 369, 467   (B) 173, 271, 369, 467, 565
    (C) 77, 177, 277, 377, 477   (D) 76, 175, 274, 373, 472

11. Find the missing terms in the below sequences

    ..., 2, ___, 18, ...

    (A) 6   (B) 4
    (C) 2   (D) 1

12. Write the explicit formula for the below number series

    2, -12, 72, -432, 2592, ...

13. If $P(A) = \dfrac{13}{20}$ $P(A \text{ and } B) = \dfrac{13}{50}$ then $P(B) = $?

    (A) $\dfrac{3}{20}$ (B) $\dfrac{2}{5}$
    (C) $\dfrac{1}{2}$ (D) $\dfrac{33}{80}$

14. An acid solution was made by mixing 4 fl.oz. of a 58% acid solution and 2 fl. oz. of a 28% acid solution. What is the concentration of the mixture?

   (A)   41%   (B)   10%

   (C)   55%   (D)   48%

15. Ship X leaves the Pier two hours before ship Y. They travel in opposite directions. Ship Y travels at a speed of 10 mi/h for two hours, at this time both ships are 120 mi apart Find the speed of ship X.

   (A)   30 mi/h   (B)   10 mi/h

   (C)   16 mi/h   (D)   25 mi/h

16. Aysha can pick forty piles of strawberries in 11 hours. Misha can do the same in 14 hours. How long will it take them if they worked together ?

   (A)   4.87 hours   (B)   6.16 hours

   (C)   7.5 hours   (D)   6.79 hours

17. A bag contains five red marbles and seven blue marbles. Another bag contains five green marbles and five yellow marbles. Jade randomly picks one marble from each bag. Find the probability of picking a blue and a yellow marble ?

   (A) $\dfrac{14}{33}$ (B) $\dfrac{7}{24}$

   (C) $\dfrac{1}{16}$ (D) $\dfrac{1}{36}$

18. A magic bag contains five puzzles and eight video games. Henry picks up an item and then another without returning the former. Find the probability of him picking puzzles in both times ?

   (A) $\dfrac{24}{91}$ (B) $\dfrac{5}{39}$

   (C) $\dfrac{4}{15}$ (D) $\dfrac{1}{6}$

19. If 33 men can do a piece of work in 15 days by working for 8 hours then find in how many days 44 men can do the same work by working 6 hours a day?

    (A)   15 days   (B)   18 days

    (C)   20 days   (D)   12 days

20. Siya, Tom and Rita invested in the ratio of 4: 7: 9. After 6 months, Siya invested $ 5000 more and after 2 months, Rita withdraws $ 7500. Find the initial investment of Tom, if the share of Siya, Tom and Rita is in the ratio of 17: 28: 35 ?

    (A) $ 70000   (B) $ 35000

    (C) $ 48000   (D) $ 66000

21. Two machines X and Y takes 2 inputs and produce one output which is greatest of all. Machine Z takes the outputs of machines X and Y as inputs. Machine Z multiplies its inputs and produces it as ouput. Based on the given information and the below figure find the missing value ?

    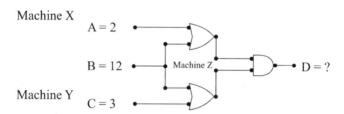

    (A)   12   (B)   24

    (C)   17   (D)   144

22. Evaluate the below series

    $$a_1 = -3, \ a_8 = 384, \ r = -2$$

    (A)   -1   (B)   221

    (C)   255   (D)   230

23. Find the number of terms in the series given below

    $$\sum_{i=1}^{n} (8m + 2) = 648$$

    (A)   15   (B)   10

    (C)   12   (D)   13

Quant Q TJHSST

Practice Test - 6

24. Find the number of terms in the series given below

$$\sum_{i=1}^{9} \left(\frac{-2}{3}\right)^{i-1}$$

(A) $\frac{4039}{6563}$ (B) $\frac{4036}{6563}$

(C) $\frac{4039}{6561}$ (D) $\frac{3}{5}$

25. How many unique permutations of the letters of the word **EMPATHY** can be formed ?

    (A) 5040 (B) 2640
    (C) 5420 (D) 3540

26. The figure below represents a picture frame and the shaded regions represent the actual pictures. The remaining part is the border around. If all the line segments in the figure are either horizontal or vertical and the picture are of same size. find the dimensions of the picture inside ?

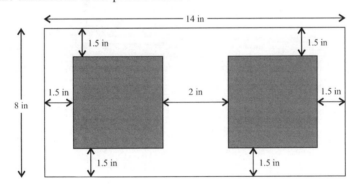

(A) 4.5 in , 5 in (B) 4.5 in , 6.5 in
(C) 5 in , 5.5 in (D) 5 in , 9 in

27. For positive numbers n , n + 1 , n + 2 , n + 4 and n + 8. The mean is how much greater than the median ?

    (A) 0 (B) 1
    (C) n + 1 (D) n + 2

28. In how many ways 8 players can be selected from a group of 12 players ?

    (A) 495 (B) 340
    (C) 120 (D) 520

Warm up 7

1. Dan can do 1/3 of the work in 5 days, Sara can do 2/5 of the work in 10 days. In how many days can both of them together complete the work?

   (A) $7\frac{3}{4}$ days (B) $8\frac{5}{6}$ days

   (C) $10\frac{7}{9}$ days (D) $9\frac{3}{8}$ days

2. Evaluate $|9x - 4| = 4$, and find the sum of the solutions

   (A) 8 (B) $-\frac{1}{9}$

   (C) $\frac{8}{9}$ (D) 7

3. Simplify $\dfrac{16}{\left(\frac{1}{64}\right)^{-n}} = \dfrac{1}{4}$. Find the value of 'n'?

   (A) 1 (B) 4

   (C) $\frac{3}{2}$ (D) 12

4. Find $(x - y)^2$ if $4x + 15y = -120$ and $11x - 15y = -105$

   (A) 11 (B) -11

   (C) 124 (D) 121

5. In how many ways 3 sales jobs can be filled from the 45 applications received for it?

   (A) 42,570 (B) 85,140

   (C) 20,770 (D) 14,190

6. Find the equation of a straight line passing through the pints G(4, −4) and perpendicular to $y = \frac{4}{7}x - 3$

   (A) $y = -\frac{1}{2}x + 3$ (B) $y = -\frac{7}{4}x + 3$

   (C) $y = -\frac{5}{4}x + 3$ (D) $y = \frac{7}{4}x + 3$

7. Albert purchased a Scrabble game at $20.50 and sells it at a 20% price increase. Find the selling price of the Scrabble game.

   (A) $4.10 (B) $24.60

   (C) $17.43 (D) $16.40

8. A minute cell divides into 5 parts every 3 minutes. In 30 minutes how many cells are formed ?

   (A) 3^{10}
   (B) 5^9
   (C) 5×10
   (D) 5^{10}

9. Best Brand store is selling TV at $362.70 which was originally priced as $604.50. What is percentage of discount offered ?

   (A) 40%
   (B) 15%
   (C) 50%
   (D) 38%

10. Sia has 5 dresses, 6 pairs of shoes and 5 hand bags. In how many ways can she dress for the party ?

    (A) 150
    (B) 30
    (C) 250
    (D) 16

11. Larry can solve forty puzzles in 15 hours. Mary can solve the same forty puzzles in 9 hours. Together they can solve the 40 puzzles in how many hours ?

    (A) 5.01 hours
    (B) 6.63 hours
    (C) 5.63 hours
    (D) 5.53 hours

12. A tiles company charges $10 per square foot. Raman wants to do tiles in four rooms of equal area in his office. If each room has an area of 140 sq ft. How much does it cost in total ?

    (A) $400
    (B) $560
    (C) $550
    (D) $5600

13. Ritvik mixes 2 Spoons of Chocolate powder for every 20 oz of milk that he drinks. If he drinks 360 oz of milk in a month, how many spoons of chocolate powder does he need for a month ?

    (A) 10
    (B) 36
    (C) 18
    (D) 72

14. Rik pulls a card from the deck of cards. What is the probability that it is a spade ?

    (A) $\frac{1}{4}$
    (B) $\frac{1}{52}$
    (C) $\frac{1}{13}$
    (D) $\frac{2}{52}$

15. When two dice are rolled. what is the probability that the sum is greater than 4 ?

    (A) $\frac{1}{6}$
    (B) $\frac{5}{9}$
    (C) $\frac{2}{9}$
    (D) $\frac{5}{6}$

Practice test 7

1. Two bus tickets from city A to B and three tickets from city A to C cost $77 but three tickets from city A to B and two tickets from city A to C cost $73. What are the fares for cities B and C from A respectively ?

   (A) $ 4, $ 23   (B) $ 13, $ 17

   (C) $ 15, $ 14   (D) $ 17, $ 13

2. The simple interest accrued on an amount of $ 15,000 at the end of two years is $2400. At the same interest rate, what will be the corresponding Compound Interest ?

   (A) $ 2496   (B) $ 2512

   (C) $ 2538   (D) $ 2474

3. Cathy purchased a bag priced at $37.95. She received a discount of 40% at the billing counter as a preferred customer. What is the selling price of the bag ?

   (A) $53.13   (B) $22.77

   (C) $36.05   (D) $15.18

4. Jill selected a X - Box for his son that is tagged with price $499.95. While paying the bill, he noticed that 6% tax is added to the tagged price. He has a store credit of $50. How much did he pay at the counter for the purchase of X - Box ?

   (A) $529.90   (B) $322.77

   (C) $479.95   (D) $630.25

5. Find the percentage change from 50 ft to 99 ft ?

   (A)   198% increase   (B)   49.5% decrease

   (C)   98% increase   (D)   26.5% increase

6. Johnson gave a personal loan to Dan an amount of $990 at 15% interest. If Dan repays it after 2 years, how much amount did Johnson received ?

   (A) $319.27   (B) $1,309.27

   (C) $1,287.00   (D) $148.50

7. Brooks gave a personal loan to Kylo an amount of $17,000 at 6% interest. compounded annually. If Kylo repays it after 2years, how much amount will Brooks receive ?

   (A) $19,081.63   (B) $19,111.79

   (C) $19,101.20   (D) $19,118.11

Quant Q TJHSST — Practice Test - 7

8. There are 12 animals in the barn. Some are ducks and some are horses. There are 34 legs in all. How many of each animal are there? How many ducks are there in the barn?

   (A) 8 ducks (B) 9 ducks
   (C) 7 ducks (D) 10 ducks

9. Find the missing terms in the below sequences

   ..., -22, ___, ___, -4, ...

   (A) -17, -12 (B) -16, -10
   (C) -19, -16 (D) -18, -14

10. Find the missing terms in the below sequences

    ..., 4, ___, ___, ___, ___, ___, 28, ...

    (A) 13, 17, 21, 25, 29 (B) 8, 12, 16, 20, 24
    (C) 12, 16, 20, 24, 28 (D) 11, 15, 19, 23, 27

11. Find the missing terms in the below sequences

    ..., 4, ___, 36, ...

    (A) 12 (B) 4
    (C) 16 (D) 1

12. Write the explicit formula for the below number series

    $3, \dfrac{5}{2}, \dfrac{7}{3}, \dfrac{9}{4}, \dfrac{11}{5}, ...$

13. If $P(A) = \dfrac{3}{10}$ $P(A \text{ and } B) = \dfrac{3}{25}$ then $P(B|A) = ?$

    (A) $\dfrac{4}{25}$ (B) $\dfrac{2}{5}$
    (C) $\dfrac{3}{10}$ (D) $\dfrac{21}{200}$

Practice Test - 7

14. Scott mixed together 5 gal. of Brand A fruit drink and 3 gal. of apple juice. Find the percent of fruit juice in Brand A if the mixture contained 50% fruit juice.

    (A) 32%   (B) 12%
    (C) 20%   (D) 35%

15. Eric started from home to Washington DC one hour before Sam left to Florida. They drove in opposite directions. Sam drove at 75 mi/h for three hours, at this time they are 485 miles apart. Find Eric's average speed.

    (A) 65 mi/h   (B) 55 mi/h
    (C) 70 mi/h   (D) 30 mi/h

16. Pam takes 15 hours to pack forty boxes of books. Kate can do the same in 12 hours. How long will it take if they work together?

    (A) 8.07 hours   (B) 7.3 hours
    (C) 7.21 hours   (D) 6.67 hours

17. A box contains five nickels and eight dimes. Marlo picks a coin and keeps it back in the box and shuffles them. Find the probability of him picking up a nickle for the first time, a dime in the second try and a nickle in the last try?

    (A) $\dfrac{1}{4}$ (B) $\dfrac{1}{16}$
    (C) $\dfrac{200}{2197}$ (D) $\dfrac{4}{15}$

18. Company X has 237 local offices and one national office and one sales office. If each local office has two CEO's and each of the other two offices has 4 CEO's how many CEO's does the company have all together?

    (A) 482   (B) 476
    (C) 239   (D) 225

19. Evaluate the sum of the below series

    $$a_1 = -4, \; a_{10} = -2048, \; r = 2$$

    (A) -4092   (B) 4844
    (C) -3777   (D) -2792

Quant Q TJHSST

Practice Test - 7

20. Bella has thirteen shirts in her closet, four blue, four green, and five red. She randomly select a shirt each day. Find the probability of her wearing blue shirt on Monday, Tuesday, and Wednesday?

   (A) $\dfrac{7}{52}$ (B) $\dfrac{1}{32}$

   (C) $\dfrac{10}{91}$ (D) $\dfrac{2}{143}$

21. A juice carton has 160 litres of Orange and Apple juice. The ratio of Orange to Apple juices is 5: 3. 40 liter of mixtures is taken out and replaced with Orange juice. Find the new ratio of Orange to Apple juices.

   (A) 9 : 25   (B) 23 : 9

   (C) 9 : 23   (D) 25 : 9

22. In Grade 8 class of RC Middle school, 3/5 of the students are girls and rest are boys. If 2/9 of the girls and 1/4 of the boys are absent today, what fraction of students are present today?

   (A) $\dfrac{17}{25}$ (B) $\dfrac{18}{49}$

   (C) $\dfrac{23}{30}$ (D) $\dfrac{23}{36}$

23. Two machines X and Y takes 2 inputs and produces one output which is product of all inputs received. Machine Z takes the outputs of machines X and Y as inputs. Machine Z multiplies its inputs and produces it as ouput. Based on the given information and the below figure find the missing value?

   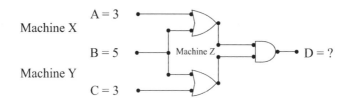

   (A) 5   (B) 15

   (C) 45   (D) 225

24. Find the number of terms in the series given below

   $$\sum_{i=1}^{n} (9i - 10) = 5320$$

   (A) 32   (B) 40

   (C) 42   (D) 35

Quant Q TJHSST

Practice Test - 7

25. Average marks of Dan in two of his science tests is 87. How many marks does he need to score in the third test to get an average of 90 ?

   (A) 92 (B) 90
   (C) 96 (D) 87

26. A plane travelled 540 miles to Virginia from Dallas. It took 6 hours to go to Virginia. It took 18 hours to travel back to Dallas due to bad weather. Find the average speed of the plane.

   (A) 35 mph (B) 60 mph
   (C) 120 mph (D) 45 mph

27. The Tiny Tots school has two branches A and B. Branch A has twelve elementary class rooms and 10 middle school class rooms with 768 students in total. Branch B has four elementary class rooms and six middle school class rooms with a total of 416 students in total. Each elementary and middle school class rooms have same number of kids. How many students are there in each of them ?

   (A) elementary class room : 14 , middle school class room : 60
   (B) elementary class room : 14 , middle school class room : 55
   (C) elementary class room : 35 , middle school class room : 45
   (D) elementary class room : 60 , middle school class room : 14

28. The figure below represents three squares A , B , C with areas of 144 , 81 , 225 sq.units respectively. A triangle is formed when the squares are joined together in such a way each square touches other two squares at one point. If D is the area of the triangle then D = ?

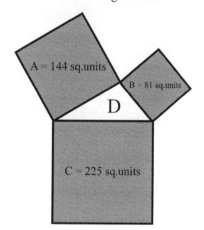

   (A) 150 (B) 144
   (C) 54 (D) 36

Quant Q TJHSST

Answer Keys

#1 Prime Factors
1. C
2. C
3. A
4. A
5. A
6. D
7. A
8. D

#2 Numerical Expressions
1. C
2. A
3. D
4. C
5. A
6. A
7. A
8. A

#3 Simplify Expressions
1. A
2. D
3. A
4. A
5. C
6. C
7. A
8. A

#4 Evaluate Expressions
1. C
2. A
3. C
4. A
5. B
6. A
7. D
8. A

#5 Exponential Expressions
1. C
2. D
3. B
4. D
5. B
6. C
7. C
8. D

#6 Distance Between 2 Points
1. A
2. B
3. A
4. B
5. B
6. D
7. C

Quant Q TJHSST

Answer Keys

#7 Midpoint
1. D
2. D
3. B
4. A
5. A
6. D
7. C
8. D

#8 Equation of a Straight line
1. C
2. B
3. C
4. D
5. B
6. D
7. A

#9 Slope (2 points)
1. A
2. B
3. B
4. C
5. A
6. C

#10 Slope intercept form
1. B
2. C
3. B
4. A
5. D
6. C
7. D

#11 Graph Slope
1. B
2. B
3. B
4. D
5. B
6. D
7. B
8. A

#12 Find the slope
1. A
2. A
3. A
4. D
5. A
6. D
7. C
8. C

Quant Q TJHSST

Answer Keys

#13 Parallel line slope
1. C
2. A
3. A
4. C
5. C
6. B
7. C
8. A

#14 Perpendicular line slope
1. A
2. B
3. B
4. D
5. B
6. A
7. A
8. A

#15 Radicals 1
1. C
2. A
3. D
4. B
5. B
6. B
7. A

#16 Radicals 2
1. B
2. C
3. A
4. C
5. B
6. B
7. C

#17 Inequalities
1. C
2. A
3. C
4. D
5. B
6. B
7. C
8. D

#18 One step word problems
1. A
2. D
3. A
4. A
5. D
6. B
7. B

Quant Q TJHSST

Answer Keys

#19 Circle area
1. D
2. A
3. D
4. B
5. A
6. C
7. C
8. C

#20 Volume of a Sphere
1. A
2. D
3. B
4. A
5. C
6. D
7. D
8. D

#21 Volume of rectangle, square, prisms
1. A
2. D
3. B
4. D
5. B
6. D
7. A
8. A

#22 Volume of cone cylinder
1. B
2. A
3. C
4. C
5. B
6. A
7. C

#23 Missing angle 1
1. B
2. D
3. D
4. A
5. A
6. C
7. C
8. B

#24 Missing angle 2
1. C
2. D
3. C
4. C
5. D
6. A
7. B
8. A

Quant Q TJHSST

Answer Keys

#25 Reflection	#26 Rotation	#27 Translation
1. A	1. C	1. B
2. D	2. B	2. C
3. D	3. A	3. B
4. B	4. D	4. B
5. D	5. B	5. A
6. B	6. C	6. A
7. B	7. B	7. D
8. C	8. C	8. C

Warm up 1

1. C
2. A
3. D
4. A
5. B
6. D
7. B
8. C
9. A
10. B
11. D
12. A
13. C
14. A
15. D

Practice test 1

1. C
2. C
3. D
4. B
5. C
6. A
7. D
8. B
9. C
10. D
11. B
12. D
13. $a_n = (-4)^{n-1}$
14. D
15. D
16. B
17. B
18. D
19. B
20. B
21. C
22. A
23. C
24. C
25. A
26. C
27. B
28. A

Quant Q TJHSST

Answer Keys

Warm up 2

1. A
2. D
3. B
4. A
5. C
6. D
7. B
8. C
9. D
10. B
11. C
12. D
13. C
14. B
15. C

Practice test 2

1. C
2. D
3. A
4. D
5. C
6. A
7. B
8. C
9. D
10. D
11. B
12. D
13. B
14. B
15. A
16. A
17. A
18. $a_n = \dfrac{(2)^n}{2n}$
19. B
20. C
21. D
22. B
23. D
24. A
25. B
26. C
27. B
28. D

Warm up 3

1. C
2. B
3. D
4. B
5. C
6. D
7. C
8. C
9. B
10. D
11. A
12. A
13. D
14. D
15. D

Practice test 3

1. A
2. C
3. C
4. C
5. D
6. C
7. C
8. B
9. D
10. B
11. $a_n = n^2 + 1$
12. B
13. B
14. C
15. C
16. D
17. C
18. B
19. A
20. D
21. B
22. B
23. A
24. A
25. D
26. B
27. A
28. D

Warm up 4

1. B
2. D
3. C
4. B
5. D
6. A
7. C
8. A
9. D
10. D
11. A
12. D
13. C
14. D
15. D

Practice test 4

1. C
2. C
3. D
4. B
5. B
6. B
7. B
8. C
9. C
10. C
11. $a_n = 6n + 27$
12. B
13. A
14. D
15. C
16. D
17. B
18. B
19. B
20. B
21. A
22. D
23. B
24. B
25. B
26. A
27. D
28. A

Warm up 5

1. A
2. B
3. D
4. D
5. C
6. D
7. A
8. C
9. C
10. A
11. B
12. B
13. D
14. B
15. A

Practice test 5

1. B
2. A
3. A
4. C
5. D
6. B
7. A
8. D
9. D
10. B
11. $a_n = \dfrac{(2)^n}{n}$
12. A
13. C
14. A
15. D
16. B
17. D
18. B
19. C
20. D
21. A
22. D
23. B
24. A
25. D
26. A
27. C
28. B

Warm up 6

1. B
2. D
3. D
4. D
5. B
6. B
7. D
8. D
9. B
10. A
11. C
12. C
13. C
14. A
15. B

Practice test 6

1. D
2. A
3. A
4. A
5. D
6. B
7. A
8. A
9. A
10. C
11. A
12. $a^n = 2(-6)^{n-1}$
13. B
14. D
15. D
16. B
17. B
18. B
19. A
20. A
21. D
22. C
23. C
24. C
25. A
26. A
27. B
28. A

Warm up 7

1. D
2. C
3. A
4. D
5. D
6. B
7. B
8. D
9. A
10. A
11. C
12. D
13. B
14. A
15. B

Practice test 7

1. B
2. A
3. D
4. C
5. C
6. C
7. C
8. C
9. B
10. B
11. A
12. $a^n = \dfrac{2n+1}{n}$
13. B
14. A
15. A
16. D
17. C
18. A
19. A
20. D
21. B
22. C
23. D
24. D
25. C
26. D
27. A
28. C

Made in the USA
Middletown, DE
24 June 2020